Greek Expectations

The Adventures of Fearless Fran in the Land of the Gods

Frances Mayes

authorHOUSE®

AuthorHouse™ UK Ltd.
500 Avebury Boulevard
Central Milton Keynes, MK9 2BE
www.authorhouse.co.uk
Phone: 08001974150

First published by AuthorHouse 11/21/2008

ISBN: 978-1-4389-3455-6 (sc)

Library of Congress Control Number: 2008910747

Printed in the United States of America
Bloomington, Indiana

This book is printed on acid-free paper.

FOREWORD

I have now spent much of my time over the last 10 years in Greece, many of the recent years working as a writer on the local English language newspaper, which I researched and wrote mostly single-handedly.

Many people have encouraged me to write about my experiences living in Greece, for they have enjoyed my stories and the way I tell them.

Well I finally decided to take up the challenge, and went back to the notes I began about 6 years before, invaluable for jogging the memory of events taking place a while ago.

I have greatly enjoyed writing the book. I hope you will enjoy joining 'Fearless Fran' on her journey of learning to cope with a beautiful country full of joys and frustrations and that gang of friendly, fun-loving individualists who are the Greeks.

ACKNOWLEDGEMENTS

I would like to thank Will who, through our delightful correspondence, inspired me to actually start writing this book, and Helena, my early editor, who put me on the right track.

My thanks to my friends Barbara, Bob, Catherine, and Hilke for their help, their feedback and their encouragement.

To fellow-authors Corinne, Lynne and Pamela my gratitude for their advice and support.

To my elder son much thanks for patient tutorials to improve my word processing skills.

To Gerry Vaughan for the use of his superb art-work

Most of all, thanks to my sister and my Dad for all that they have done to cheer me on, and the practical help they have given, in the creation of my book.

All the characters, human and animal, and the places, in this book are real, but only a few have their real names. To all the people I met in these wonderful Greek places, who made my experience what it was, *'Euxaristo poli'* - Thank you very much.

IMAGES

STARGOS

Elsie's Empire - Fran's plan. An ink drawing of the layout of Elsie's estate at the Kalivia. P 4

Nelly asleep by Fran - a pencil drawing of those stolen moments on the living room sofa P 71

Entering Elsie's Easter 99 - from a photo by Fran, showing the plum tree the bees loved. P 82

Stargos - the best beach in Greece? From a painting by Fran - a privilege to walk on this fabulous kilometre of white sand with no one else there P 94

KALKOS

Clock tower and village from a painting by Gerry Vaughan - coloured pencil, wash and ink P 114

Church tower and tree by Gerry Vaughan - pencil and ink drawing P115

Kornaros turning at dawn by Gerry Vaughan - pencil, charcoal and chalk drawing P 165

Mouthouria by Gerry Vaughan - ink drawing of the house Fran and Dad bought P 174

NAPLOS

Makrinitsa from a painting by Fran - that painting which made me miss the bus. P 216

Naplos seafront statue from a painting by Fran - watercolour pencil P 218

CHAPTER 1 - THE KALIVIA

A dog called Nelly started it all. I was new, untried in Greece, and out for a walk, in mid-November, on a Northerly headland in Stargos. I had come to the island to teach English, but was determined both to keep up my fitness and explore my new country.

Those smart Italian boots in pink imitation 'Goretex' had seemed a good idea, but in fact required numerous stops to release the build-up of steam. And it was on one of these stops that Nelly, careering down the scrubby hillside, goat bell clanging (goat bell??), found me.

Not being a natural 'dog person' I was a little alarmed, and more so to find a second dog in tow. However, Nelly exhibited 100% enthusiasm and 0% aggression towards her new friend. But the first encounter was to be fleeting. Hearing a motorbike puttering to-and- fro on the dirt road above, I looked up to see a duffle-coated and woolly-hatted figure astride, taking an interest in the proceedings.

'Aa eeyoo ohll raayeet?' enquired the figure in surprising cut glass tones. Well, this was no Greek peasant, but, from the voice timbre, a woman it seemed.

'Fine thanks, just having a rest!' I replied. 'Seem to have acquired a couple of dogs.'

'Well one of them's mine... Nelly come! COME! etc, etc....' Nelly blithely ignored all this, nosing around the bushes, and me, with her chum. By now exasperated, the figure dismounted and scrambled down the hill. Nelly was seized by her collar, and dragged, bell clanging, up to the road.

Hmm, no introductions then. I went on my way, soon to find the path was very difficult for the time left. Indeed it was almost invisible among the small scrubby heather-like bushes, and descended at such a steep incline towards the beach below that the whole idea had lost its appeal. I could see myself losing the track, or, worse, slipping, or wricking an ankle. So I abandoned my walk and set off down the long slope into Stargos Town. The only embarrassment was that Nelly's erstwhile chum, the other wretched dog, followed me all the way (but not to my flat, thank goodness) and I could not suppress a pang of guilt that the poor creature would have a long walk home, and that, probably, there was some other puzzled owner out searching.

With the worsening of the weather, I did not attempt the walk again, though I had found more social pursuits through the 'Ladies Association', a sort of 'ex-pats WI' (men welcome as visitors) which met weekly in the Scout hut. This edifice was quite well-appointed but absolutely freezing cold in the winter months, so some hapless volunteer was designated each week to go in an hour early, in suitable layers of insulated clothing, and make a log fire in the large fireplace, to ensure some comfort for the members.

And 'twas at one of these meetings, some weeks later,

in January, that I, strolling back from getting a coffee, heard those cut glass tones from the hillside encounter. Homing in, I found Andrew, one of the British husbands, in conversation with a striking figure. Elsie was tall, rangy, silver-haired, and evidently patrician in accent and demeanour. Once introductions were made, Elsie, who rarely came to these gatherings, revealed her mission.

'I have this advertisement to put up to find someone who can live in my house over the winter. I go back to London to research my book on the History of Stargos.'

Ignoring the meaningful looks which Andrew was beaming forth, I was immediately gripped. Here was a fascinating idea, an opportunity to be grasped. I (Fearless Fran to some) had never been one to shrink from adventure. So...

'I think I would be interested. Tell me more about it.'

'Well I think I need to know a bit about you first.'

And so in the course of the conversation the dog with the goat bell got mentioned, and it emerged that it had been myself who had so attracted Nelly on the hillside. Elsie was radiant.

'Goodness if Nelly liked you like that we must give this a try! When can you come up?'

I could hardly wait for Saturday afternoon, when, released from teaching, I was able to ascend the hill once more, on foot again, as I had not quite sussed out the bus yet, but better prepared this time for the baying hounds who deafeningly defended every house I had to pass. Why do the owners want them? Surely the barking drives them crazy. And the poor dogs, how bored they must be. Little wonder they go berserk when they see someone (As you can see, I am, at this point, as yet very inexperienced in Greek ways, and especially unfamiliar with the constant need for noise).

Upon reaching 'the Kalivia', as this upper collection of settlements was called, my perspective on the landscape altered, as I was focussing this time on Elsie's estate, which backed on to what had seemed an unremarkable dirt track a month before. The estate was cunningly built into a slight escarpment, the back of all the buildings to the prevailing wind. The long verandah in front of the line of rooms was charmingly arranged in an I-shape, enclosing the garden, but also affording a fabulous view over the valley below (containing the airport) and over the sea to the neighbouring island.

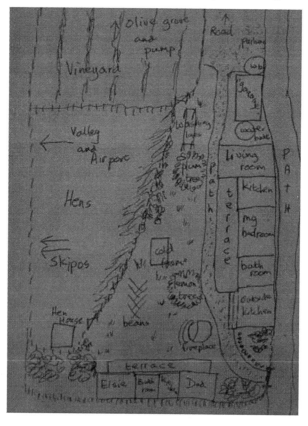

I instantly took the place to my heart, becoming more excited with each fascinating new feature – wood-burning stoves, cats, hens, vineyard - and anxious in case Elsie would not take me on. The 'interview' seemed to be going well, but there was one aspect which I was dreading - tackling the car. There was no way I could do the job at Elsie's, and still manage my teaching job, without it. But …

'Here you are, the car keys. Go off and have a test drive!' cried Elsie happily.

My stomach flipped with nerves, but I proceeded determinedly to the little ex-rental Yugo, and hoped Elsie had not noticed me trying to get in the 'wrong' side. That was it. I had never driven a left hand drive car before, nor driven on the right. And this road, though not busy, was a bit hairy.

'Well, best get on with it and get it over with,' I muttered grimly to myself.

Either I am a better driver than I gave myself credit for, or the little car was very forgiving, but, in good order, I got as far as the bottom of the steep escarpment just on the northern edge of Stargos Town, stopping short of venturing where there was too much other traffic - yet.

Better get back. She'll be wondering where I've got to. Aah! This hill's a bit steep. And there's the bend just before - can't get up speed, but second must be ok. Hmm… Oh No! Stalled. Got to roll back. What if something's coming??!! Best get moving. Too steep for second it seems, up in first….. Phew!!

I managed to look reasonably calm when I returned, to find Elsie expansive, and ready to move to the next stage, which was to have me read through the journals, over about

16 years, which previous tenants had written. Obviously I was about to join a long line of former incumbents. But, among the rural idyll, my attention was suddenly riveted by the tale of an unfortunate woman who had had an accident while changing a petro-gas bottle and whose injuries proved fatal.

Well, this was a testing moment. Time to pay special attention to what petro-gas duties were likely to be in view! Of course, the kitchen had a cylinder, and so did the outside kitchen where the pet food was prepared. With a leap of faith in my ability to cope when the time came, I quietly resolved to do as much cooking as possible on the wood-burning stoves. There were several varieties of them, 2 with marvellous ovens for stewing chicken etc while at work, and hotplates for keeping the kettle boiling throughout the evening.

But this pet food thing…I had never had a dog, but was pretty sure that I would have fed one on tins from the supermarket. And then there were the 2 cats, Charlie and Anna, ditto. So it was a bit of a surprise to learn of a substance called 'dog macaroni' which came in huge sacks and had to be boiled up in a huge cauldron with interesting additions - bones from the butcher (or an occasional treat of chicken livers), lemon, garlic, and *horta* (leaves looking like dandelion but tasting a bit like spinach). Tins were only for emergency back up.

The hens were a simple matter, handfuls of corn twice a day, but of course there was the cockerel to be wary of. And the enclosure looked a bit large, but then I was no expert on such livestock. Elsie warned of the continuing problem of the hens getting out, and wondered if I might find a solution. Thank goodness Elsie had got rid of the donkey she used to have!

For Elsie (a Londoner by birth and still in possession of her father's house in Kensington, her winter home) had arrived on the island in 1968 and proceeded to acquire a hut on the hillside, and a donkey. She had to live at first with no water or electricity laid on, gradually buying land and building further prefab-like structures tacked onto each other, to form the eventual I-shape.

So what other duties would I have? Well, there were seeds to be planted, and a frame for the beans to be constructed. The arrival of the Winter wood supply had to be dealt with. The *yiotresi* (the well pump) had to be run occasionally, up in the olive grove. *Horta* for the animal food (and human if desired) was plentiful in the rows of the vineyard. And, the dreaded petro-gas had to be purchased, and the bottles exchanged. Well at least the place had a phone to summon help if necessary.

This could also be used to get in touch with Elsie, at her Kensington address, but only in an emergency, because of the expense. Mind you, I would be paying the phone bill for the period of my stay. Most of the time, we would write to each other. I would have charge of Elsie's Post Office box key. So I would need to check on any important mail, bills etc and deal with them as appropriate. I must admit, I was having difficulty imagining Elsie, despite her evident education and breeding, suddenly transported from her rustic Greek island isolation into the bustle of the UK capital. Still, perhaps it was this annual injection of city living which kept her sane, putting both ways of life into perspective. And how I dealt with the rustic environment would be documented, for another responsibility was to record life at the estate, in the current volume of the journal.

'....And any other improvements you can make...' said Elsie, casually.

At these words, the creative spirit in me stirred. Here was a remit to prove my practical ingenuity, a chance to 'make a difference', a challenge to my 'wombling' skills.

The deal was struck, which did not involve payment for me, just the chance to use the estate and car. Dates were agreed, when I would move in, overlapping slightly with Elsie, whom I would drive to the hydrofoil. It was a little disquieting for me, though, when I returned from work on the eve of Elsie's departure (early rising essential) to find the said departee falling down drunk on *ouzo*.

'Aaah....Ffraaahncesss....Ffoood!' Elsie cried, lurching dangerously towards the stove, stumbling down inches from the hot metal, before scrambling back to the sofa. I extracted the casserole, and, unable to banish the image of an insensible Elsie, unrousable in the morning, warily picked at the meal. Luckily, Elsie staggered off to bed relatively soon, leaving a worried Frances to try for some sleep.

Well, at 5.45 next morning, before the dawn, I was amazed to find Elsie bustling about her final preparations, bright-eyed and bushy-tailed. They do say that if you stick to *ouzo* or *raki* (the schnapps or grappa of Greece) and don't mix your drinks, you don't get hung over. But, clearly, the level of intake Elsie could handle would have flattened most strong men. That takes serious practice. Awed, but relieved, I took my place, in the growing light, behind the wheel, and soon delivered a slightly emotional Elsie to the harbour-front. Amid pledges to write, to phone, she was aboard, and gone.

And I was left to reflect on the coming new phase of my life, and what had led up to it.

CHAPTER 2 - HEADING FOR GREECE

I had recently qualified in Teaching English as a Foreign Language, and, having been let down over a planned job in Prague, had chosen Stargos, and Sofia, over a less appealing position in the industrial hinterland of the Czech Republic. When the agency contacted me I dithered at first, keeping my options open, but when Sofia rang Edinburgh in late October to make a direct appeal, we hit if off immediately, and I was won over.

It seemed that Sofia had engaged a native speaker as a teacher, a PhD no less, who unfortunately turned out to be an alcoholic. Her consumption of a few gins for Dutch courage before facing the kids did not long escape the notice of the Greek parents. So, suddenly, she had to be thrown out, and Sofia was left without a teacher to take over from Anastasia, who was pregnant. Sofia was delighted to agree terms with me, but really wanted me over as soon as possible. But I was adamant about a certain date in November, for I had something important to do first.

There was a certain girls' school in Edinburgh, portrayed by Muriel Spark in 'The Prime of Miss Jean Brodie' as 'Marcia

Blaine'. I had, in 1968, joined the ranks of former pupils of this formidable but highly esteemed and academically productive institution. And lo, they had chosen the 6th of November that year for their 30 year reunion. I would rather have submitted to dentistry without drugs than missed this. Especially as I was now able to pull off a glamorous, slim, blonde appearance as opposed to the rather chubby mousiness I had exhibited in 6th Form. I was going to sock it to 'em! Turning up at the hotel in my floaty frock and high-heeled sandals, I was confronted with a curious effect. Half of the people there looked almost identical to how they had at school, while the other half were totally unrecognisable. And I was slightly miffed that people knew who I was.

Still, one can take this to mean that one has not aged much from one's youth, I comforted myself. Kay, my pal, whispered while posing for the group photo,

'Well, we're wearing better than most of this lot!'

And as if the blonde glamour were not enough, I proceeded to win the school-memories-related quiz (bizarre prize, a giant Easter egg). Furthermore, when everyone heard about the flight to Greece early the next day, I was awarded the title of 'Shirley Valentine' (of course). Curiously, prophetically maybe, I had attended the World Premiere of the film in summer 1989 at the Edinburgh Film Festival – and emerged crying

'I'm only 39 and I can do ANYTHING!'

So it was with the good wishes of my old school friends, and the inspiration of Shirley, patron saint of ex-pat women of a 'certain age' that, on 7th November 1998, I boarded the Easyjet flight to Luton, and thence onward to Athens. There,

Sofia had arranged a small hotel near Syntagma Square, handy for the bus which would take me northwards in the morning to the port for the Stargos hydrofoil. I resembled a large Christmas tree, with bags of all shapes and sizes dangling off my body, and a large suitcase to boot; there were complications over what I had to bring with me. First, there were the English books. Even though Sofia assured me that she had all sorts, I felt the need for some of my own, as a security blanket (one that cost me £60 in excess baggage mind you). Then there was this holiday, at Christmas time, a cruise which had been booked over a year before, when I was still teaching in Primary school in England. Well, cruises, as we all know, are quite dressy affairs, and therefore I had been forced to pack some rather glamorous attire, and a bit of 'bling', which would not normally have featured among my 'Winter in Greece' wardrobe. But there was no time to return to Edinburgh for re-packing before flying to London to join my father and my sons. We would then fly to Rome to join a ship which would later call in (ironically) at Athens.

So there I was, heading for Greece on 2 fronts. But how did it all come about? Born in Edinburgh in 1950, my whole Education was there, till I left University, in 1972, an English Graduate about to attend Liverpool Polytechnic to gain a Postgraduate Certificate in Librarianship. My sister Margaret, 3½ years younger, was following the same path behind me, though destined for a good career in the computing sphere. At Library college, I met Peter, formed a relationship, and, by the end of the course, got engaged. We ended up living in London for 2 years, marrying in January 1974, then moved to Merseyside where I worked as a Teaching Practice Librarian.

(It seems Teaching was already putting out tendrils to pull me in.) After a few years, Peter wanted to move on, and despite only just finishing doing up our Edwardian semi, we had to move across country to Teesside.

I was very pregnant with our first son, Thomas, and of course had to leave my job. By the time we found a house, in a lovely Georgian Market town south of Middlesbrough, and were able to move out of the accommodation the Council provided, the baby was due any day. But luckily he decided to arrive 11 days late, giving me just time to decorate the nursery. Life settled down, though the death of my mother, in 1981, from cancer, was a huge sadness, not only for the loss of her lively, funny warm creative self but also for the fact that she only knew her first grandchild as a year-old baby, and never her others, James, born in 1982 and my sister's children Andrew and Elizabeth, born at the end of the 80s.

Naturally, my sister and I were worried about my father, who had nursed my mother in her final weeks, and who was now retired and left alone. But he embarked on a new life (hmm, does it run in the family?) by going to University, which he had missed out on as a young man. He qualified BD but being past retiring age could not hope for regular employment as a minister. He proceeded to do a further degree with the Open University, then, still not academically exhausted, went back to do a general degree at Edinburgh. During these years, he visited us a lot, and took enormous delight in Thomas and later in James. I was never ideally suited to be the mother of small children, finding the circles I was in rather frustrating. So I was glad to get a temporary job as a librarian at a Further Education College in 1986. We also moved house that Summer, to a lovely (but un-modernised) bungalow in a quiet cul-de-sac close to town. While I was at the college, I noticed a course in Teaching English as a Foreign Language, but it seemed very difficult to get a place. My friend Morag had done TEFL straight from University, lived in all sorts of exotic places and then settled into seniority in the TEFL world. I shelved the idea, for with a young family its time had not come, but went on to take a fateful decision.

Because one of my friends was doing teacher training, and because it seemed a logical job for a woman with school age children, I applied. I was accepted, at the University of Durham, for a year-long Postgraduate course in Primary School Teaching. (There was no way I was going to tackle Secondary pupils).

Now when I was at school, even in the supposedly ground-breaking 60s, there were few careers open to clever but unexceptional girls. One had to be very clever for Medicine, yet Nursing was beneath one. Art required outstanding talent to have any chance of success, similarly, Acting. In both of these I had some promise, but had to be realistic about my prospects of earning a living. Teaching was very usual, though secretarial work regarded as only for academic low-rankers. Well I was no doctor in the making, though I flirted with the idea of being a radiographer. So I was left with Teaching, or what I chose, Librarianship. I had decided while at school that I was temperamentally unsuited to teaching. However, these worries could be put aside, surely, now that I was 20 years older and had my own small children. Well, things went all right at first, at the learning stage in College, where I performed well. But later, in schools, I was plagued with self-doubt and nerves, leading to problems. Of course, the fact that my marriage had collapsed was undoubtedly a factor.

My father was staying with us to be our child minder, allowing me to commute to Durham and Peter to work. With both of the boys at school, Dad was in charge of taking them and bringing them home. This would have been a happy time except that the increasing tension between Peter and myself was not improved by our attendance (too little too late) at Marriage Guidance.

December 1987 saw a crisis, with Peter saying he was going to have to leave. Stunned though I was, I managed to turn things so that I went off to live in Durham so that I could complete my course, while Peter, my estranged husband was left with my father and my sons in Yorkshire. Well my Dad was a trouper, only really discomfited when having to witness the visits of Carol, the woman who had befriended me to get close to Peter, and learn our secrets from me. Carol had obviously been instrumental in Peter's decision to leave me, for she now had him for herself. Yes, that is one of my faults, and I do not seem to learn with experience. I am far too open and trusting, especially with other women, whom, naively, I believe to be 'on the same side'. But this was, as my father had spotted, 'a dangerous woman'. Peter did find this out during a holiday, and dumped her.

Needless to say, our home town was soon abuzz with the gossip that I had left Peter, so I was branded the guilty party. My decision had been that the only way that I could cope with finishing the course was to leave. I had judged that the stress of commuting and looking after Dad and the boys as well as the work for the course would be too much. I had told our boys that Daddy and I did not want to live together any more. Thomas, at 7½ , understood, and cried for a while, but little James, just 5½, could not grasp it.

Without making too long a story of it, I moved to Durham, to a block with nice people, came home at the weekend, and passed the coursework. But I fell at the last fence - my Final Teaching Practice. The stress of what had become an emotional roller coaster in my marriage left me unable to cope with the demands of the teaching and I was really quite ill with it all. But, in the light of my good general performance, and full of sympathy for a trauma they could not take into account in marking me, the University allowed me, in the Autumn, to repeat the practice. This time I passed, and was now on the road to getting work as a teacher. But it was a visit to Sheffield, to Peter's oldest friend, Liz, that changed the track of my life once more.

I had been to London for a reunion with some of my pals from the PGCE course, and was on my way back, calling in at Liz and Dave's house, which we had visited as a family in happier times. My self-esteem had been so low that I was ready to be painted out of the life in North Yorkshire, be bought out of the house (for a small sum as I now see) and lose the custody of my sons. Liz took stock of this and immediately urged me to get back in the family house, and that Peter could not stop me. So I did, he moved out (after a horrendous month of cohabitation) and I went back to living with my boys.

I had, of course, missed the probationary intake for that teaching year, but Peter was supportive, with very good maintenance until I could find work. In a long process, I finally got work as a supply teacher. Indeed, I did my probation as a supply. This was unusual, but successful, cobbling together periods of service from various schools. It was from the last that I got a job in the 'wrong' school for me (so my wise senior colleague told me).

But to cut a long story short, she was right, and I was shoved around that school from one age group, and classroom, to another. Eventually, my health and my confidence in pieces, I had to leave. Better experiences followed, till finally I fell foul of political forces at another school and decided Primary School Teaching and I had had enough of each other. It is ironic that during all that, I was studying for various courses, and emerged with a Science diploma, an MA in Education and training as a Nursery Inspector. Furthermore, I was a veteran of no less than 4 successful Ofsted inspections in 8 years. (I kept running into them on these temporary jobs.)

Out of a job, and with a mortgage, other debts, and 2 children to support, I could have settled for a clerical job or some such. But out of the embers of my teaching career emerged at least the semblance of a phoenix. I remembered about TEFL. Realising I had a month after the Summer when I was still being paid, I enrolled for the 4 week intensive course at Windsor. Happily, I was able to stay with my sister and her family in Reading. And so, successful, I emerged qualified in October 1998, but once again having missed the start of the teaching year. However, by later that month, enter Sofia and Stargos. My aim was to do a couple of years abroad to 'win my spurs' then retreat to the UK and enter the teacher education field. People had often asked me why I was not teaching adults or 6th Formers. I needed motivated learners who were prepared to listen to what I had to offer.

But what of my children, now teenagers? For 10 years we lived in our lovely bungalow in Yorkshire, the boys seeing their father regularly, mid-week and every second weekend. Peter had a house nearby, a new partner (whom he had met in the early 80s) and now a half brother, Gary, for Thomas and James. As for me, I had only one liaison which I could even begin to call a relationship. But, hats off to you Dominic for your great company and what you did to keep my boys amused while I was busy studying. The years of my boys growing up into teenagers were probably the happiest of my life. They revelled in each other's company, while Peter and I worked hard to cooperate successfully to give them a balanced life with both parents. Thomas and James were, and are, loving and funny, clever and helpful, good-looking and honest - indeed as splendid a pair of human beings as one could wish for as one's children. And I missed them. And I still do.

By September 1998, when I left for my course, Thomas was about to go to Birmingham University. James was in the first year of 6th Form. Since his father lived not far from the school, and James was used to staying there (and got on well with Gary), it seemed the natural thing for James to go and live with Peter. It was something I had talked to him about, that he might want to go and live with his Dad at some point. The fact that things did not work out for James in his later schooling is a constant pang of guilt for me, wondering if he felt I abandoned him, and it dragged him down. Peter, close to the situation, reassured me that it would have happened anyway. As you can see, we all get along pretty well for a 'broken' family. Sometimes I joke, though maybe I should not, that I am not a middle-aged woman suffering from 'empty nest syndrome'. I flew the nest before they did.

Returning from Windsor, and knowing I would be leaving for abroad, I rented out the house. After a brief sojourn in Edinburgh, courtesy of my wonderful Aunt Moira, I wowed it to the old girls of 'Marcia Blaine', and took off for Greece. But of course I was already destined to go there, having booked the 'Ancient Wonders' Christmas cruise over a year before. And it was on that cruise that my father fell in love with Rhodes, thus paving the way for his connection with Greece to grow stronger.

CHAPTER 3 - FRONTISTIRIO

Sofia was somewhat taken aback at the sight of me staggering off the hydrofoil with all my stuff, but somehow piled it all into the borrowed car, and set off for the little apartment she had rented for her employee. Normally the place was let to tourists in the Summer, but this Winter let to teachers was a handy extra earner for the owner. It was 10 minutes walk from work, clean, well furnished, with cooking facilities, a nice shower room, and a sunny balcony with bougainvillea. Suitably impressed, I settled in happily, and set off later to visit the *frontistirio* (tutorial college) where I would be teaching classes as the 'native speaker'. Now of course at this stage I spoke not a word of Greek –except having learned '*parakalo*' and '*efharisto*' (please and thank you). Best to learn to be polite from the word go, when in a foreign land.

Sofia was adamant that I should never attempt to communicate with the children in Greek, as they would run rings round me, thus making a fool of me, losing respect for me, and damaging discipline all round. This made a lot of sense, especially as my Achilles heel as a teacher had always been the discipline angle. (As it turned out, later, when the children got to know me, I would occasionally try out bits of Greek I had learned, and the children would encourage me.) In these TEFL courses, the teachers have to be trained to teach English IN English. After all, faced with a class comprising a Turk, a Swede, a Spaniard an Italian and a Japanese, one could hardly be expected to teach every one of them in their own language.

On my course in Windsor, the class had been taught Portuguese IN Portuguese, a language none of us knew, to let us see what it would feel like. It was interesting how the class divided into the slow set, the defensive ones and the 'have a go' types (I myself being one of the latter).

And yes, I wanted to learn Greek . And I found a teacher, one Thassoula, who taught private pupils at her house. The only drawback was Thassoula's habit of staying out in the clubs and bars half the night drinking tequila shots, thereby failing to be awake even at noon or 1 o' clock, when the eager pupil turned up. So the lessons could be sporadic affairs. But, particularly given the poor example of my predecessor, there could be no such dereliction of propriety in me, when faced with my pupils.

Nothing stronger than coffee was ever consumed on the premises. I was bemused, however, on my first visit, to be offered coffee and then presented with a beaker and a jar of coffee and some sugar and shown the water tap.

'But, what am I supposed to do with these?' I enquired.

Sofia and Anastasia looked at each other. Both shrugged.

'Well I guess it's hot coffee time again,' said Sofia.

I had had my first meeting with that curious instant coffee concoction, the *'frappe'*, usually whipped up to a froth with a machine, available (normally black) in various strengths from *sketo* (no sugar) to *gliko* (wince-makingly sweet). But, it being nearly mid-November, it was judged that Winter could be said to have arrived, and the filter machine chugged into action.

After a couple of days familiarising myself with the books I would work with, and the routines, and having sat in on classes by both Sofia and Anastasia, it was time to take on the classes by myself (always with the reassurance of Sofia in the next door classroom, ready to read the riot act if things got out of hand.) While I was used to children in numbers, Greek children in whatever numbers are a formidable prospect. They are brought up to be super-confident, and out for themselves, with an impatience, and a volume, to intimidate the average well-meaning educator.

But, why all this extra-curricular tuition? This seemed peculiar to me as a UK person, where extra tuition for our schoolchildren is an unusual phenomenon, usually related to a special exam or a specific disability. However, as I discovered, Greek schoolchildren typically can attend as many as 3 extra courses of an afternoon and evening (eg Maths, English and French). School in Greece only , certainly in those days, only opened in the morning from about 8.15 to about 1.30 at the latest. And that time would be interrupted by playtime. So how on earth would they get through everything? thought I, as an experienced Primary School teacher familiar with the struggle to cover everything within a UK timetable, Well one answer is that Greek education is very prescriptive, very didactic. The books are set and, in theory, all children in a certain school year should be doing the same lesson on the same day throughout Greece. This is rote learning, which has to be spouted back to the examiners to a suitable standard for the child to be allowed to progress to the next class up. So children can be held back behind their peers.

Although afternoon sessions in the Greek schools are not unknown, it is not for every pupil across the board, and only in certain subjects eg Maths. The upshot of all this is that the Greek parents (those who can afford it) pay for their children to do more in certain subjects, which presumably also has the useful benefit of keeping the children occupied, out of harm's way, and out of the parents' hair at home. (Not to mention the benefit to families where mother and father both work) Hmm, *frontistirio* as childminder? I never thought of that before.

Of course, it is not all English teaching, for one can learn German, French, Maths etc depending on the scope of the school. But English is by far the commonest subject taught. And English is very important in Modern Greece, for it is the international language of tourism, the most important industry for the country. Apparently, since about 2001, anyone starting to work with tourists is required to have passed an English qualification equivalent at least to First Certificate. This, though well above elementary, is not a high grade qualification like the American Michigan Certificate or its much more difficult companion the Cambridge (which I have to say few British A level students could pass!). Therefore, English is a great asset to a young Greek setting out for work in whatever sphere, and hence the enthusiasm for learning it. Sadly, from the point of view of people like myself, they seem to have zero interest in teaching anyone their own native language, and

Greek is challenging to pick up as you go along.

The set-up at Sofia's *frontistirio* was a ground floor entrance directly from the narrow back street, passable only by bikes not cars, into a corridor going through to the back area which housed the staff workroom and the toilet. The classrooms, which were arranged with the blackboard walls 'back to back' both sat to the left of the corridor. The windows were high, to give privacy and avoid distractions from outside. The décor was very plain, with the odd poster (usually an advert for a series of textbooks) relieving the plainness of the tired white walls. The floors were marble tiles, the desks bench-type, in rows. I usually taught in the front classroom, for the back one had the phone and so it was better for Sofia to be there.

To me, used to carpets and central heating, the ambience seemed very chilly, though the presence of legions of young bodies had usually warmed the place up in the hours before I arrived to teach. Everywhere there were books, on shelves round the top of the blackboard, and more shelves all over the walls of the staff area. Sofia was not kidding about having lots. But I actually worked with a fairly restricted range of books - and lessons within them. Over many years, Sofia had tried and tested many texts, and identified the ones which worked best.

Of course, my classes were the ones judged to be already competent enough in English to be able to understand me at all. Sofia herself, and Anastasia until she left for her maternity leave, taught the 'babies' who needed everything explained in Greek. Sofia was very disparaging about her own Greek, though I was in awe of anyone who could speak it. It was an amusing moment though, when my sister Margaret phoned up from the UK and proceeded to speak Greek to Sofia. The only trouble was, Margaret only knew Ancient Greek, which definitely fazed Sofia somewhat. On the odd occasion, I was brought in as a sort of 'guest' into these classes of younger children, for Sofia rightly thought that it was a good thing to expose them to a 'real' native speaker. She, as an American, was very pleased with the contrast between us. Furthermore, Anastasia praised me as being very clear in my speech - a benefit, I am sure, of being Scottish, for the well-educated Scots tend to pronounce words very literally, and with not too extreme an accent.

It was a cultural education to find myself in front of a sea of faces all apparently shouting at once *'kiri! kiri!'* with lots of arm-waving and bouncing up and down thrown in. Well, with some amusement, I identified this mysterious appellation as short for *kiria,* the word for a lady, which also does duty as a title - Kiria Mayes presumably standing for Mrs or Miss Mayes (or even Ms as I went though a phase of styling myself). Peter would have been Kirios - Mr Mayes, or, in school, 'Sir!

Not only were the younger classes boisterous, but they lacked in what I considered to be common standards of politeness. It was a continual uphill struggle to instil into them that if they wanted something they had to say 'Please can I have?' rather than the ubiquitous and peremptory 'I want'. It was a little while into my Greek classes with Thassoula before the penny dropped that Greeks do not normally use 'qualified' expressions such as 'I would like'. The equivalent in a restaurant, say, of 'What would you like?' is 'What do you want?' To a British person of course, a child saying to a teacher ' I want a pencil ' or whatever, seems rude, arrogant and so on. And of course I set about making sure they behaved otherwise. But, from my initial outrage, I progressed to a bit more cultural understanding. I have no doubt that national reputations are won or lost on such matters.

Another interesting view is that national characteristics follow the character of the language. Well Greek is certainly direct, no prevarication there. They have so many different words that they can get a very precise meaning, but often they are lazy and use the same word for different things, as English never would: eg 'foot' and 'leg' and (disconcertingly) 'separated' and 'divorced'. The Greek language is very difficult for foreigners to deal with. Yes, Greeks are direct, and they can be lazy. They admit themselves - and their Government feels the strain of it - that they are a nation of individuals. Greeks pursue their own interests with a tunnel vision which appears to ignore the rights of others, but basically means that they are assuming 'the others' are doing the same. The British, the nation of deference and expertise in disciplined queuing, find the Greeks pushy and rude. The Greeks find the reserve of the British puzzling, and the vagueness of English annoying. Linguistically, they dislike conditionals, and trip up especially on prepositions and phrasal verbs like 'put on', 'get by.'

Generally though, the classes behaved well for me, though I used to get exasperated with the Michigan (a high level exam) class composed mainly of teenage boys, whom I once accused of suffering from 'testosterone poisoning'. Although I had brought up 2 sons, they did not behave like this! I was wading through my first encounter with the sexually-charged 'super ego' of the Greek male.

With Sofia, I was very helpful, staying behind to do marking, and generally impressing with my attitude. Sofia in her turn was very helpful to me in negotiations with authorities, and booking of flights etc.

One of the most eye-opening and amusing episodes was the visit to the health centre, in order for me to have my medical check and x-ray to allow me to register officially for teaching. Sofia in the lead, we entered the modern- looking medical centre behind the town's central road. The first thing I saw was a doctor in a white coat leaning on the front desk, smoking. Hmm, this was unusual behaviour, utterly foreign to British experience.

There then began processes which later were to become familiar to this British neophyte. Sofia and I, beginning the trail with person 1, were sent off to an office to get a piece of paper stamped by person 2, then back to person 1 who then sent us to person 3 for another stamp. Person 3 proved to be a very tall, well-built man clad in a lumberjack shirt, who, despite his size, was apparently devoid of enough spit to lick a stamp, for he had to make a great performance of moseying off to the sink to fill up his little sponge container for stamp-wetting before moseying unhurriedly back, and settling down to give the required endorsement. Impatience fought with amusement in me, while Sofia (an American Greek fed up with the local ways) made cynical comments *sotto voce.*

Finally, after the to-ing and fro-ing, we teachers reached the inner sanctum containing 3 doctors, gathered together (which spoke of under-employment - but at least none of them was smoking.) The one in charge, a seriously gorgeous young man, proceeded to give my all-too-willing anatomy the once over, while discussing with his colleagues (in Greek of course translated to me by Sofia) the matter of my chest x-ray.

Doc 1:-'So now she must have an x-ray!'

Doc 2:-'She does not need one.'

Doc 1:-'...But she does! She is a teacher.'

Doc 2:-'Well she can't have one!'

Doc 1 'Why not?'

Doc 3:- ' (whispered aside) ..Er, the x-ray machine's broken.'

Doc 1:- (to Sofia) '...ah, um, It will not be necessary for her to have an x-ray!'

Sofia was nearly choking with mirth, translating this, while trying to appear respectful to the doctors, whose cooperation, after all, she needed. So a diagnosis by eye had to suffice to decide that my chest (not large, but perfectly-formed) passed muster for the ranks of the teaching profession.

Ah, but when it came to my qualifications, further ghastly ramifications of bureaucracy lay in wait. My degree scroll was written in Latin, but had to be translated into Greek, but only by an officially recognised translator, of course, not the helpful school teacher who had a go, and had his efforts rejected. Then it all had to go to some office in Athens, to be pored over by a number of stamp-happy 'jobsworths', before being returned, ratified, and suitably garlanded with red tape. By the time this was done, and Sofia applied to register me, she was told it was too late for that year. So I remained an illegal teacher (not for want of trying to be otherwise, and unnecessarily paying IKA national insurance). I had to be hidden or passed off as a visitor if the tax people were in the offing.

I was happily settled into a routine at a school I liked, where I got on well with the boss. This alone made a nice change from some of the horrors of my UK primary school career. The children worked well, were lively but never nasty, often quite the reverse. I was startled one night, when writing on the board, clad in the striking outfit of pink chenille baggy jumper, dark green leggings and bright pink climbing boots (plus matching slouch socks). Suddenly a voice from the front row behind me announced, 'I think you are very beautiful.' I was a bit non-plussed, not least because the owner of the voice was a rather attractive lad. I just mumbled, 'Well thanks,' smiled weakly, and went on. Privately, I was thinking, Blast! First man to pay me a compliment here, and he is 'off limits'. On my perambulations around the town though, I had been meeting others.

CHAPTER 4 - GETTING TO KNOW YOU

In downtown Stargos, fairly handy for the *frontistirio,* there was the lovely taverna to which Sofia and I would repair every second Monday, Sofia's treat. I learned the delights of *kalamari,* here in its stuffed form (like a strange fishy cannelloni). We were able to share our histories of ending up on Stargos, while I was also able to study my companion in a more relaxed setting than the school. Sofia's family had originally been from Stargos, and indeed it was her grandparents' old house that she inhabited. Her father had emigrated to New York, and married into the Greek community there, but daughter Sofia, observing that there were other brothers and sisters around to care (eventually) for the old folk, and disenchanted with the pressures of New York, elected to come over to the island. A match was made between her and Kostas, though it seemed a pretty fiery relationship, Sofia frequently complaining of him being ' an asshole' - and indeed Kostas eventually admitting as much and trying to make amends. I never dared to enquire what his 'asshole' behaviour entailed. Other women? Staying out late? Being inconsiderate? Violence? - no. Best not to ask.

I would say now with hindsight that Sofia was very much an American; outspoken, charming, go-getting (all good Greek qualities too, admittedly) but not compliant with the accepted male-female balance. In traditional Greek homes, the wife has to stay in the domestic sphere, at her house or those of friends and family. Her freedom to see whom she wants, when she wants, where she wants, is much circumscribed. In turn, she rules the house, and is free to scream at her men-folk to gain their obedience.

Now there may well have been a clash here between Kosta's view of how an island wife should be, and Sofia's Americanised attitude to marriage, as a partnership, with neither party under the other's control. And of course Sofia, under pressure at the school, had no choice really but to be a workaholic, which was a likely cause of trouble with Kostas.

It may just be some conventional prejudice in me, but I could never quite imagine them as a couple though, for Kostas was dark and wiry, and not very tall. Sofia, by contrast, was about the same height as him, and well-covered - a UK 18 I would say. She had quite a dark complexion, a largish nose, beautiful brown eyes, and lovely thick curly hair, changing from pepper and salt to all grey. This premature greyness, common in very dark-haired people like the Greeks, is absolutely stunning against their honey-coloured skin. But best of all was her lively character, with a great sense of fun. She sustained her energy all afternoon with coffee and cigarettes, and the temptation to join in was irresistible. I can make any excuses I like, but as a 'stranger in a strange land' I was all too likely to seize upon any comforting habits, bad or good, that I could find.

So getting to know Greece and Sofia had put me back in the toils of one of my worst vices - smoking; not an easy thing to overcome at the best of times, but in Greece, a nightmare. Although less so than in my first years, smoking is still pretty ubiquitous, with no 'out of sight out of mind' advantage, nor any 'smokers as social outcasts' propaganda to stiffen the resolve. But at least I did not use alcohol to prop up my confidence, so avoiding the fate of my predecessor.

Around the town of Stargos, the shops were mostly in the modern main street, while the most attractive part of town was the West side, where the old houses climbed up to a headland. I got a bit of a crush on Stelios, who ran a gift shop selling polished stones, and boldly left him a note asking him out for a drink. I am a direct sort of girl, but shy with it, you see. Thassoula was horrified at this behaviour. Well, Stelios was evidently not interested, luckily for me, for I later discovered that the object of my interest had not only been running a brothel, but also making soft porn videos at the said establishment. It seemed his wife had 'shopped' him to the police. Ok, so he proved not a great character to associate with.

Vangelis at the central grocery store was definitely an ageing *kamaki* (Greek version of a gigolo) from the Rayban sunglasses right down to the cowboy boots. But he had a lot of charm, and encouraged me to try out my first stumbling words in Greek. It took me a while to get the hang of Greek shop hours, supermarkets being the exception to the rule that one opened in the morning, then closed down for a long period in the hot afternoon, re-opening in the evening. Given my enthusiasm for shopping, it is just as well that this timing meant I was usually busy up at the estate or at work when the shops were open. Nevertheless, I got round quite a lot. I patronised the religious artefacts emporium for what I termed a 'dingly-dangly thing' i.e. one of the glass vessels suspended on chains, used in Greek churches as oil burning lamps. Up in the back streets of the West side, I found a marvellous pottery shop, and bought various sets of drinking vessels and jugs, although slightly uneasy about how they were to be transported safely to their eventual destination.

The jewellery store also saw a little business. Irresistible in the window was a still-treasured turquoise and gold necklet, delicately worked with several dangling ornaments. Further 'must have' apparel, especially as the weather got warmer, was the easy cotton clothing, loose tops and drawstring-waisted trousers, which found perfect partners in my new 'gladiator' sandals, really like little ankle boots made out of leather strips, with a zip up the back. At the posh underwear shop, I acquired a 3- piece set of leopard skin and black pyjamas and robe, in stretch velour - so 'cheesy' it was almost elegant.

Well, it was a very Greek elegance, for I was beginning to notice a few things about Greek women, the way they dressed, and their appearance overall. There was a definite age divide. One very noticeable feature among the younger age group was the general tendency to wear clothing that was at least one size too small, leading to what one could have been (flatteringly) called 'body conscious' sexy dressing, but which in fact resulted in decidedly unaesthetic sights, even among the slimmer exponents. Yes folks, the Greeks invented the 'muffin top'. As to what their trousers were doing to other parts of their anatomy, it brought tears to my eyes just to imagine it. Studying the faces, there was surprisingly little heavy eye makeup, but this was well 'made up for' by a bizarre attraction to lip-liner, usually the particularly unappealing look of pale lipstick with darker liner. (Was this ever in fashion?) One had to admit that they looked what a Northern European woman would consider to be a bit 'tarty'.

A favourite with the older ladies was 'big hair', going well with their lasting affection for that other 1980s phenomenon, large shoulder pads. Without resorting to uncharacteristic sartorial behaviour, one way of making myself look more Greek was to acquire a pair of serious sunglasses. Consequently, I invested in a rather swanky pair of heavy tortoiseshell ones from the opticians, which I decided gave me a definite exotic glamour. For that was it. Greek style was over-the-top glamour, and I decided I was going to rather enjoy that.

On a more serious note, about 3 weeks into my stay Sofia decided it would be a good thing for me to experience a visit to a Greek Orthodox church, so we agreed that on the coming Sunday morning we would meet up and attend at least part of the service. These services go on for nearly 3 hours, so it is quite common for people to drift in and out, or just show up for the communion part. As it happened, the Sunday we had chosen was far from typical, for it was a memorial service, a remembrance of someone who had been dead 40 days. This would be the first of a series, at various intervals, culminating in the 3 year memorial. So it was a very solemn occasion, I feeling slightly embarrassed to be there (though I suppose anyone can attend someone's funeral if they wish). What was more poignant was that it was the memorial for the father of one of our pupils, Thomas, a well-grown lad of about 15. He looked very much the man of the house in his smart grey suit.

But he struggled to retain his composure. Although feeling like a voyeuristic interloper, I could not help but be fascinated by the rituals, and by what appeared to be an ornately decorated white cake, displayed in the centre of things.

After the service finished, we all slowly filed out, to be met with presentations of the contents of this 'cake' which was in fact boiled wheat, sweetened, portions of which were scooped into bags for those attending the service. Sofia contrived to stay for a chat, and we were treated to Greek coffee (which I still can't get to like) and, rather unusually, brandy. This was my first taste of Metaxa, the deceptively delicious Greek spirit with a vicious after-kick. I am ashamed to say I sampled everything with gusto, as it was all new and intriguing.

Life fell into a comforting routine, with my work (mostly evenings, but with a couple of afternoons and Saturday morning) affording me time for exploring the town and the island, and pursuing craft activities, ever a hobby of mine. In the run-up to Christmas, I was happily employed in my spare time making cards and workbooks for sale at the Ladies Association Christmas Fair. I discovered the fascinating properties of the bougainvillea flower, which hardly needs to be dried, as it comes off the tree already resembling tissue paper, and formed the 3-D decoration on many of the cards I produced. In the event, my stuff did not sell too well, but the cakes and the mulled wine contributed by the German contingent were great, while the Dutch produced the most amazing waffles.

At the Christmas Fair, I met a lovely American couple, Martha and Bill, who had been away in the States but recently returned to Stargos. We got chatting and soon I was delighted to be invited to see their lovely home, high up among the old streets on the West side of town. They had a terrific collection of books, and a computer, with access to email if I wanted it. Their house was full of lovely artefacts they had picked up around Greece, particularly carved wood and hand-woven tapestries. On the roof terrace, with its fantastic views, we ate and drank and I counted myself lucky to be in a place where one could do this in Winter - and to be their grateful guest.

Martha and Bill had embraced Greek cuisine enthusiastically, and we dined on excellent olives, *dolmades* (stuffed vines leaves) and *mousaka,* a layered dish of minced lamb, aubergines and béchamel sauce. I had long been a fan of olives - especially the luscious black Kalamata ones - and had often made *mousaka,* though not usually with the classic lamb mince, but with beef. (This is probably sacrilege - but then historically beef is less common than lamb in Greece). Also, in some strange prophetic way, in the December of 1987, in the middle of my teaching course, and with my marriage poised to break up, I had chosen to make Greek food for an international buffet at college. I laboured long over the *dolmades,* remarkably fiddly as they are, and even longer over the *baklava.* This unbelievably calorific concoction of *filo* pastry, nuts, syrup and melted butter looked the part, but I had over-boiled the syrup so nobody managed to get their teeth through its concrete-like texture, but had to fall back on admiring its authentic appearance.

It is an interesting point to note that the Greeks' Mediterranean diet with its high vegetable and fish ingredient, as well as the ubiquitous olive oil, includes them among one of the lowest rated nations for heart disease - and this despite the practically compulsory smoking. They are not a nation of drinkers, believing (very sensibly) that one should not drink without food, and thus looking disparagingly askance at the British and other Northern European tourists who indulge in a bevy of 'g and ts' or whatever, before going anywhere near dinner. However, mitigating against all this worthiness is their enormous consumption of bread (the highest consumption per capita in the world), and their equal fondness for sweet things.   Heart disease may be relatively low among the Greeks, but diabetes, of the situational late onset variety, is very common.

Greek cakes are incredibly sweet, and come in a number of varieties. There is the huge gateau type, composed of what appears to be cream layered on cream layered on cream (in fact confectioner's custard which has the amazing property of being both creamy in texture but firm enough to hold a shape.) Then there is the bewildering array of pastry concoctions whether with flat *filo* or the shredded variety in *kataifi*. Nuts, dried or stewed fruit, and syrup are the normal fillings and additions to these rolls and slices and parcels. Less known but equally deadly are the chocolate truffle type, literally like large chocolates, and often wrapped in foil. And I have not even started on the biscuits, but certainly if there were ever a rival for my Granny's shortbread, it would be found here.

Early on in my stay in Greece it occurred to me that what appealed to me about the country was a certain semblance to Scotland. Both countries have rugged terrain, covered in hardy bushes like heather, and grazed by sheep (or, in Greece anyway, goats). Rocky mountains, often snow-covered, with skiing; a plethora of islands. Both have an economy originally based on small farming and fishing (leading to an abundance of photogenic fishing boats), but now mainly dependent on tourism; a national costume featuring men in skirts; a musical tradition embracing both fiddle (in Greece the *lyra)* and pipes; a fondness for fiery local brews (and furthermore, interestingly, a shared liking for whisky - the most popular spirit in Greece).

The inhabitants of Greece and Scotland, both EU extremities, exhibit a fierce national pride, but the indigenous population is far outnumbered by ex-pat nationals who emigrated. Like many small nations, both the Greeks and the Scots have 'chips on their shoulders' about being bullied by more powerful countries. Admittedly, the Scots take a more serious approach to life, and are good planners and organisers, not a Greek strength. Where the Greeks are strong is in individual self-confidence and National self-esteem, not wasting any time on the Scottish pursuits of over-analysing and self-deprecation. The people agree in their love of sweet sticky cakes. The Greeks' sweetmeats are more sophisticated, but they would still find comfort in Scotland, where there are often more bakeries in any street than anything else. But the Scots, sadly, do not share the Greeks' nutritional magic, and have about the highest heart disease rates in Europe, no doubt as a result of a marked preference for pie and chips over Greek salad.

Certainly, this Scot, never a pie and chip fan, largely owing to continually 'watching my weight' was enjoying the different foods to try, and the abundance of vegetables which actually tasted of something. I had always found tomatoes a waste of time, but Greek tomatoes were a revelation. And then there were all these different varieties of olives to try. I was surprised indeed to find that porridge oats were readily available in Greek supermarkets - yet another link with Scotland. But 2 things especially intrigued me.

Firstly, I noticed a super-abundance of pulses like beans, split peas, lentils, chick peas in the shops. Now I had imagined, as many would who knew Greek cuisine largely by reputation, that the Greeks ate salad, *mousaka*, kebabs, fish, lamb chops and such like all the time. Well, the first is certainly part of the daily diet, but the others would be restricted, for 2 reasons. The first is economic. Meat is a more expensive form of protein, and it is not that long since Greece was a poor nation. The second is religious, for the strict Orthodox observers would spend many days of the year (Lent being the main period) abstaining from meat, oil, dairy products in varying degrees of privation. Many people now just give up meat for Lent. But an alternative protein source was necessary, hence the abundance of pulses, and some wonderful recipes to go with them.

The other fascinating culinary phenomenon was this stuff called *manna*. Well I was immediately back in the desert with Moses when I heard this name. It seems as if the Ancient Hebrew word was adopted straight into Greek when the old texts were being translated to form the first books of the Old Testament, in Ancient Greek. In any event, this stuff hardly resembled ordinary bread. It was usually brown, like wholemeal bread (though white variants exist), and resembled completely dried up small rolls - large rusks really. This dried bread is designed to be added to other foods for bulking out purposes. Thus, having made a soup or stew, the housewife would add some of these which would then soften and mix in. *Manna* has its origin on Crete, where one wonders if the particular characteristics of the island led the inhabitants to find it convenient to be able to store large quantities of dehydrated bread against the unavailability of the fresh kind.

I like to dip mine in my soup, though not mix it in, rather like dunking a biscuit. The rusk would pleasantly absorb the liquid. And one had to do this. Anyone unwise enough to set off with a couple of rusks of *manna* instead of their normal crispbread to have with their lunchtime cottage cheese would very likely soon be calling the dentist. Another delightful way of enjoying them, and keeping my hands off tempting sweetmeats, was to dip them in my (low calorie) hot chocolate. At that time, this was something that I could not buy in Greece, so my luggage would always feature a few jars, and all visitors would be asked to bring some, along with the decent teabags and the Marmite.

CHAPTER 5 - FIRST EXPLORATIONS

The weeks up till Christmas saw me undertake not only the walk which lead to my life changing meeting with Nelly and Elsie, but another walk, one which (like Topsy) 'just growed'.

Setting off from the town, at the Eastern end of the island, I proceeded to walk and walk, till finally, after 16 increasingly weary kilometres, I reached the island's most famous beach, almost at the Western end. The trouble was, I had forgotten to bring any water (not something I would worry about on a Scottish winter walk, though maybe I should). What led me on and on was the conviction that, surely, somewhere along the coastal road I was following (a very busy strip in the season), I would find a shop of some sort open - but no. It was out of season - and Sunday. Well, it was only luck that placed me, exhausted and with a piercing dehydration headache, at the bus stop, just in time to get one of the few buses that day making the trip back along to town. It was a miserably chastened creature that groaned her way back to the flat.

What had made the lack of water worse was another daft mistake of the innocent in Greece. Observing at the side of the road an olive tree bearing black fruit (one of my great loves for years) I proceeded to pick one to have a taste. Well, reader, if you have never done this - don't. Olives fresh from the tree are disgusting - hard, and bitter in a persistently lingering way reminiscent of that bitter aloes stuff one uses to stop nail-biting. Goodness knows how the Greeks, or whoever first cured them, discovered that they have to be soaked in brine for ages. Probably some street-wise peasant living near the sea observed the contrast between the original item (very unpromising) and the ones which had accidentally fallen into the sea. And so a delicacy was born which turns out to be one of the healthiest foodstuffs one can have.

Sofia, her plump frame clad habitually in jeans and sweatshirt, had been a bit scathing about the 'bling' attire required for the cruise, expressing hopes that nothing sparkling would be worn to school. But she was a good sport about helping to fix up my flights to return to UK for this holiday. Then there was the question of a suitcase. My large one had 'expired' on reaching the flat, so another must be found. Nothing suitable was available on Stargos, so a date was fixed for a trip to the bigger shops of the mainland. But come the day, a Saturday morning in early December, the heavens opened and I experienced my first serious torrential Mediterranean Winter downpour. Not only were the two of us soaked, but the hydrofoil was called off. Gloomily, Sofia already fretting about the cold her wet feet would bring on, we washed-out travellers sploshed our way up the flooded streets to Sofia's house for a welcome coffee. So began regular visits to Sofia's comfortable house, where husband Kostas would occasionally put in an appearance, and from whom I learned to make an excellent shrimp pilaff.

In the matter of the suitcase, I was disappointed. With time running out, necessity made me vow to make the trip - alone - the following week. Luckily, the mainland city, Naplos, proved a relatively easy one to deal with, the main streets being arranged in a grid pattern inland and uphill from a long attractive seafront full of cafes, handy for the hydrofoil mooring. I managed to find a suitcase, which of course hampered my exploring from then on. But I was proud to have tackled a strange Greek city with success.

When it came to getting around Stargos, I soon discovered a number of things about Greek towns and streets. One was the almost total lack of pavements. One simply just had to walk in the road. And in the Winter these roads were frequently a couple of inches deep in water, drains not being one of the features of Modern (as opposed to Ancient) Greece. So the famous pink Goretex boots were a godsend as I could splosh my way along to work, trussed up like 'Nanook of the South' as I used to joke with Sofia, damp above but dry in the feet region. This made for an unusual classroom look, but it seemed to go along with my rather 'funky' image as far as the pupils were concerned.

At first, I had to beware of traffic, as I had not got used to the 'driving on the right' thing, and would look the wrong way. Many of the roads were very narrow, and should really have been one way. But the Greek drivers managed in their typically anarchic fashion, as I would later learn to do. But as for eccentric motoring behaviour, it would take a lot to beat the family I saw at the supermarket near the edge of town.

This was an eye-opener, especially shocking to one newly-arrived from the controlled, safety-conscious environment of the UK. The Greek attitude to personal transport, and personal safety, and the relationship between the two was to be perfectly encapsulated in my observation of this family on their way home from the supermarket. Dad, well built and over 6 foot, clad in a red boilersuit, and his wife, not much smaller, emerged bearing 8 bulging carrier bags, and an accompanying retinue of 3 children ranging from about 9 down to 3.

Astonishingly, they arranged themselves (not a helmet amongst them) with the practised ease of the motorcyclists at the Royal Tournament, atop a 100cc moped. Mum was behind Dad, holding 3 carrier bags each side, the 2 older children balanced, one on each side on the foot plate, holding the handle bars, and a carrier bag each, while the youngest child sat in front of Dad between his legs, as he somehow balanced and steered the whole precarious crew on the poor little protesting bike. I could only stand and gawp, and reflect on the likely nature of the road accident statistics in Stargos (rather alarming as it happens, especially involving inexperienced foreigners on hired motorbikes, a fact the Greek authorities were anxious to conceal).

I wandered all over the town, which was basically divided East West with the more modern Eastern side built on flat land, of unappealing concrete. Here were the holiday apartment blocks, similar to the one I inhabited. A road ran along the seafront from the harbour area out to the airport in the valley to the East. This airport was notorious in Greece for having a lethally short runway. One mistake and the plane would be in the sea. (One imagines a similar problem, on a larger scale, in Hong Kong) So, two things had to happen.

Firstly, the pilots who would be flying in and out of Stargos in the season used to come and practice landing and taking off: Reassuring, that. Secondly, the international planes going North used to take off with only enough fuel to get to Thessaloniki, where they would refuel with a full payload. This did lead to hilarious mistakes on the announcement screen, however, when someone had got the columns wrong on the computer, and had all these planes going to Thessaloniki via Gatwick, Oslo or wherever.

Around the airport were a number of creeks, with, surprisingly to me, what appeared to be bamboo growing along them. Was this a native plant? Had it been introduced from the Far East, which is where I perceived it as growing? It was certainly useful for making into the temporary bamboo shade roofs used on pergolas, on beach bars for example. But the developments along the shore on the edge of town were more than beach bars. There were some large clubs, and pleasant apartment blocks, leading into the area where the bars, motorcycle hire shops, shipping agents, etc had their premises. There were not many restaurants in the Eastern end, mainly large bars and cafes, set out with phalanxes of comfortably-cushioned cane chairs under the pergolas.

Across the road, the land rose quite quickly into the cobbled streets of the old western part of town, where the restaurants tended to congregate. This is a feature of Greek life, which I first noticed in Athens. Shops of certain types tended to cluster together eg all the lighting shops, furniture shops etc. This is fine if all you want is lighting or furniture, but what if you want all sorts of things? And I could never quite understand what their theory must be about competition. Certainly, if one has the time and energy, one can compare goods and prices in all the shops, but frankly, I prefer a street where I can get all the different things I might need. I suppose the practice has its origins in the historical phenomenon of 'quarters'. The only one I know in the UK that is not a specialist centralised market like Covent Garden is the Gold Quarter in Birmingham, where it is a bit startling to see armed guards patrolling around the neat little redbrick streets. For all I know there are other survivors of this ancient way of organising businesses.

So the land on the West rose up to the headland, overlooking the fish market, the extreme eastern end of the harbour-front. And up in the back streets were mainly private house, with a few restaurants or individual shops, such as the one where I bought pottery. The nightclubs were centred mainly on the first street back from the main road, one of the streets which did not really allow cars except for cautious loading access on the widest of them. But motorbikes were a different matter. Sofia came to work on hers, largely because of all the books for marking she had to carry, rather than the distance (which would have been a shamingly short journey).

In the middle of the harbour-front, where the road through the town emerged, and converged at a roundabout with the coastal road, there was the landing stage for ferries and hydrofoils, with a large drop off car park. Beyond this, there was a causeway seaward out to the large fort which occupied an islet in the sea. These rather neatly, and in a picturesque manner, divided the commercial harbour from the fishing harbour, as well as giving Stargos's seafront a pleasing texture and distinctive appearance.

Always, on my meanderings, I was on the lookout

for suitable locations for doing artwork. I had brought my watercolour paints, and was looking forward to capturing various scenes. One rewarding painting, which I had to do very quickly, captured the old buildings of the high western headland. I had to lay it all down wet on wet, with the last orange and yellow rays silhouetting the outline changing and fading. (I have since mislaid this painting, a source of great annoyance). Another good location was the little cove next to the cemetery.

Cemeteries in Greece do seem to be placed in locations with fabulous views, as if those photographs of the dead on the tombstone (also found in Italy) are actually able to see and enjoy it. But the best painting I did was of the western harbour-front, where a blue and white painted bar sat framed by the trees and houses behind, next to the colourful fish market with its attendant fishing boats. On the few occasions when I visit my father's sister-in-law, I can pause to study the painting, which I gave her as a present.

The weeks up till the Christmas break passed quickly, with Sofia booking my flight with Easyjet over the phone. So began the next stage, getting packed for the holiday, the 'bling' attire cluttering up my wardrobe at last coming into its own. In the event, despite nearly missing the flight for Rome, my father, my sons and I all had a wonderful time on this Christmas cruise of the Eastern Mediterranean and Holy Land. After Rome and Naples, the ship called in at Athens, and was later to call at Rhodes. It was the attraction of the latter and my father's love for the place which was to have another influence on my future.

But Athens, merely glimpsed as a portion of Syntagma

Square before, duly impressed, with trips to the Acropolis and to Sounion. Apart from a bit of jewellery, the only thing I bought in the 'tourist area' of Plaka was a book, an unusual book, and one which was to cause a furore in the Greek media a few months later. And so we digress, to discuss the subject of that book, and a study area naturally of interest to me - Greek men.

CHAPTER 6 - GREEK MEN

The anonymous author of that funny and daring book, 'Greek Men Made Simple' included certain subtitles. 'Everything you ever wanted to know PLUS everything you never thought to ask', and 'A beginner's guide to the Greek male'.

Wow this looks interesting - and amusing, thought I. But the furore in the media puzzled me. Well, the Greeks claimed that the book was insulting both to Greek men and women. But, of course, those in the know (especially readers of the book) could simply turn to page 19.

'Greeks are very uncomfortable with the English sense of humour and are very afraid that you could be laughing at them.'

And then, of the islanders (not the more sophisticated city Greeks)

(They) 'think the rest of the world is scared and jealous of the Greeks', and also believe the Americans to have a special 'get the Greeks' department, 'cooking up schemes'. Page 89.

I found it so beautifully ironic that the very fact that the Greeks got so aerated over this tongue-in-cheek, ultimately affectionate send-up proves one of book's central points - that the Greeks have no sense of humour against themselves. In a society where image is all, anything appearing to puncture such posing is taken as a serious threat. Humour in Greece, I have found, seems to be very much of the physical kind, or based on farce, (as any Greek soap opera will confirm). It is not witty and verbal in foundation. (Aristophanes and Euripides must be twirling in their graves). And how did I find the book useful? Well, a lasting lesson, which reverberated through the years, was the attitude to women (aka 'pussies' in the book) on their own. To quote page 55,

'Greeks are brought up to think the worst thing that can happen to you is to be on your own. It's amazing how uncomfortable pussies who live happily on their own make them.'

I met surprisingly accusatory attitudes to being on my own.

'Why are you? We must find someone for you!'

In vain might I protest that (a) I had not yet found the right person and (b) I was not in a rush to pair up with just anyone for the sake of doing it. I was to find that there were many men who assumed that they would automatically be welcomed with open arms for their generosity in offering to keep me company at night (but of course never being around when really needed, as in when I was struggling off the boat with lots of shopping.)

I was most amused by the passage which explains the Greek male's 'excessive use of reflective surfaces'. To quote from pages 4 - 5.

'All Greeks have a very short shelf life and the

transition stage from beautiful Adonis to old fat and crinkly is spontaneous. Take a look around you in Greece, beautiful young men and short, fat balding optimists. Nothing in between, one second beautiful, the next ready for the recycling plant. This spontaneous combustion leads to constant fear and insecurity in the male population. They must make the most of what they have while it's still functioning.'

So checking his reflection every 30 seconds is important.

Another habitual activity of the Greek male is 'undercarriage checking.' All men are hugely in thrall to the interests of their dicks, but in the Greek male it is as if he merely co-habits his trousers with this (p11)

'separate life force over which he has no control (therefore anything it does is not his fault). He must consequently spend much time re-arranging it and generally keeping it happy.'

This of course has a dual purpose, both ensuring that the guiding force of his life, the being which leads him down the street, is all right, and, also, drawing the attention of any passing 'pussy' to it.

Soon, I started spotting 'types'. Well, an easy one was Vangelis in the supermarket, with his leather jacket, white t-shirt tucked into crotch-padded jeans, slicked back hair and cowboy boots - classic '*kamaki*' gear. (*Kamaki* is literally 'harpoon' – a rather Freudian image of young men 'spearing' as many girls as possible) The trouble was, Vangelis, pushing forty, was balding and his stomach was getting ahead of the rest of him, so it was not an appealing look.

Then there was the ghastly man who literally hi-jacked

my suitcase in Syntagma, insisting on taking it to my hotel. To my dismay, the room clerk did not protect me, so I found myself upstairs in the room with this man. I managed to get out of there for a combination of reasons. Firstly, the man (early 60s at the youngest), despite playing the strong man, was sweating and puffing so much that I was worried about him. Clearly he was not fit enough to overpower me. But just in case, I agreed to have coffee with him, to get out of there fast. Now, as I was later to discover, going for any sort of refreshment with a Greek man is regarded as striking a bargain in which the goods on offer are oneself. Page 27 says

'Let's have a coffee' is code for 'I want to have sex with you'.

However, it turned out that this fellow, clearly past it in the '*kamaki*' arena, was of another classic type. As described on page 27 in the NAF (Not awfully fantastic) chat-up lines section.

"Come and work with me' Offer of job working in real estate office, travel agency, etc etc. the idea being, in return for about £300 a month you can be available for 'free' sex. Ugly, middle aged men, to be found everywhere in Greece.

Really? You think I would go within 10 yards of you for that much money? (well any amount of money but ten pounds per day???) Do I look so desperate? I better get a new beautician when I get home.'

Well, I did get a phone call from this guy later in the day, but managed to choke him off. Meanwhile, Sofia, who was checking my progress back from the Christmas cruise, was horrified to hear what had occurred.

And then, on a day trip to another island by hydrofoil,

I encountered a real *kamaki* type, who favoured me with what 'Greek Men' (page 8) calls the 'I want to fuck you silly look', accompanied by a bit of classic posing, in this case the one leg up on a step to increase emphasis on crotch bulge. I maintained an impression of insouciance during the voyage, knowing that this guy would expect me to get off the hydrofoil at the first port, to get the bus to Athens. But I was staying on for my trip. I chortled inwardly as he hung around the bus, not wanting to choose his seat till I settled myself, then, dismayed when I did not appear, had to board the bus at the last moment.

Away from the *kamaki* types (who consider themselves REAL men), there are the 'real real men', the ordinary souls who do not get involved with tourists. Now it was quite likely that the young lads at the school were destined to be the nice boys whom 'Greek Men' talks about (p39), not pursuers of tourists (though many go through a brief phase of this). They tend to be shy and not inclined to frequent tourist discos etc. They will have real jobs. They are the targets for the nice Greek daughters (not often allowed out in public, and certainly not alone) who are paraded in the '*volta*'. And so, obsessed as they are about whom they are going to marry, they may well find someone there, posing with everyone else in their best clothes.

Other types of Greek men are described on p37-8. Older Greek men may well be lawyers, doctors, etc in the 'cuddly professional' category, the favourite prey of Greek women, being respectable, reliable, and well off. Thus foreign women rarely get a look in. The good-looking poseur, the rich playboy and the gambler are recommended for a fling, while 'the philosopher' describes the head of the family in his dominant position, taking up as much space as possible on his central chair, expounding his stress-free, woman-loving approach to life.

The trouble is that, as the book claims (page 3), any woman coming on holiday to Greece is doing so in order to have sex with a Greek man . Apparently, it is useless to protest that one was attracted by beautiful beaches, great food, interesting sights. 5 million Greek men can't be wrong. I discovered early that, while as a middle-aged woman in the UK, I was invisible to men, Greek men would react quite differently. I could certainly tell I had arrived in Greece because, immediately, at the airport I was being openly stared at by every variety of Greek male.

This is partly because all Greeks are very nosy about other people (expect to be asked how much you earn, how much you paid for your house etc within minutes of meeting them). But it is also partly because of a macho 'right' to look upon women as objects for men's entertainment. And then of course (page 13)

'his self-esteem depends on having every woman in the room wanting him'.

I was initially pleased and flattered, until I heard, and worked out, that I was not being admired for myself, as special, but as a female to be used. Furthermore, I bore in mind the incredulity of the men about women living alone.

In Greece, in Winter, with few tourists around, the testosterone level reaches the danger zone, and thus the criteria for choosing a mate are expanded to include any female willing and still breathing. Well, one might say, why is it so crucial to have tourists around, for the Greek men to have a sex life? It is not that easy for Greek men to have sexual relationships with their own race, for young girls are being protected by their families, preserved for marriage. And many of the young men who pursue tourists are Greek women rejects, not up to scratch for whatever reason, and, so, dependent on foreigners.

Greek culture seems to the outsider a curious mixture of matriarchy and misogyny. The most powerful figure in a man's life is his mother, and the only creature he fears is a Greek woman. And yet, the freedom of women is severely curtailed. The book (p41) speaks of the limited female role models Greek men have to identify with - basically, virgin, mother or whore. Once married you have to take on the role of a mother. (page 15)

'I didn't realise that living in a matriarchy actually meant I had to be my man's mother...'

But the following joke is all too true (p41)

'Q. Why did the Greek boy think he was Christ? A. He thought his mother was a virgin and she thought he was a God.'

Greek mothers have a lot to answer for in terms of breeding a race of male supremacists. But, confusingly, the recommended ways to handle Greek men are very schizophrenic. A sample from page 24...

1. Treat them badly.   2. Do not love or respect them.

4. Screw them senseless   5. Be unpredictable.

6. Be honest. This is because almost all Greeks lie all the time, so honesty completely throws them.

11. Work out how to make them jealous and insecure,

whilst at the same time convincing them they possess you totally.

Or, put another way... page 15

'be unavailable but totally unable to live for five seconds without him, be totally inexperienced about the ways of the world, but the hottest thing on two legs, be gentle and reassuring but very strict and difficult, make him chase after you whilst demanding marriage at the same time.'

Phew! I thought after studying this. It all sounds too difficult, quite beyond me! But, of course, I was to get involved with Greek men, and sadly to forget all the advice in the book eg about not falling in love. For, as the author sums up on p.96, despite their 'short shelf life', while Greek men are at their best, they have

'the most wonderful smiles on the planet' and 'eyes to melt even Thatcher's heart'.

CHAPTER 7 - OUT AND ABOUT

On my return from holiday, I arrived at Athens airport in the late evening, and resolved to go and wait at the bus station in the city until the early bus left in the morning. It was well seen that I had little knowledge either of the nature of the bus station nor of the area around it. Not only does it not stay open overnight but it is in one of the least salubrious parts of Athens. My taxi driver, who spoke little English, but was obviously a very decent guy, became very concerned about dropping me off in such a spot, for he obviously knew I would be prey to every low life character around, the area being near Omonoia, centre of drug and criminal dealing in Athens.

I felt as if I was being kidnapped by this driver, who, having let me see the bus station from the outside, insisted on shooting off somewhere else, with me as a helpless and anxious captive passenger. As it turned out, he had been trying to think of somewhere handy and relatively safe where he could deposit me in what was now the early hours of the morning. It turned out to be an all night café, peopled by rather strange but seemingly harmless characters. Here, at 3 am, I fed my bemused stomach some rather greasy lamb stew and proceeded to occupy myself with some marking of compositions which I had take away with me so as not to let my usefulness to Sofia slip too much.

Come the dawn, I set off in another taxi to tackle the bus station. And I was shocked to find what a truly ghastly place it was. I often joke that it was as if one of those design teams from the TV makeover shows had been sent with the remit to make the place as dirty, tasteless, sleazy, unsanitary and uncomfortable as they could. From the dirty floor to the poor lighting; from the ripped orange vinyl seating to the truly unspeakable toilets; from the dingy blue paintwork to the positively Dickensian coffee bar it really was the nastiest place I had ever been. The couple of hours I had to kill before my bus were torture but I survived it and the coffee. On my return to Stargos, Sofia was not only unimpressed with my independent efforts to move myself around Greece, but alarmed at my risk-taking. And I was later to find she was determined to trump what she saw as my disregard for my own safety.

After the holiday, it was time to pack up again, for the move to Elsie's. Luckily, I was able to use the car, and had soon unloaded everything into the large bedroom next to the kitchen. This was also handy for the living room and bathroom, and rejoiced in a wood-burning stove. I could not understand why Elsie did not have this room for herself, but she preferred the other end of the 'I-shape, and used 'my' room mainly as a library,

Now Sofia was of course a little put out at my arrangement with Elsie, possibly wondering why she was still paying for the flat in town. But in fact I was determined that the flat should be kept. After all, it was costing Sofia no more whether I stayed in it or not - and it would be important if I were to have a social life in town. In reality, it was my dependence on Sofia for company and entertainment which was most likely at the back of it. I had demonstrated an ability to find a niche for myself, which side-stepped Sofia's role as guide and mentor. As I have said, Sofia, for reasons of work, and husband, was an entertaining but infrequent companion socially. Nor would her companionship be offered in some of the more adventurous activities I wanted to sample. Sofia, for reasons of energy conservation partly, was a bit of a 'couch potato' in her free moments.

But almost before I had begun to settle into life at Elsie's, a sad event occurred, at the end of January 1999. My dearly loved Aunt Moira, who had helped me so much over my difficulties with storing clothes and papers when renting out my house, had died suddenly. I would have to go back for the funeral, and to arrange what was to happen to my possessions when the house was sold. Thank goodness Elsie had made provision for what was to happen in the event that I was indisposed or unavailable. She had arranged with her nearest neighbour, an Englishwoman married to a Greek, that she would look after the place. I felt a bit awkward having to ask her, but she was fine about it, and said she sometimes fed the animals and kept an eye on the place if Elsie was away for a few days.

Poor Sofia, having only just got me back after Christmas, and getting into our stride in the new term, sprang loyally into action, and I was soon on my way, this time via Amsterdam with KLM. While I was in Scotland, I had to sell my car, which was parked on the drive at my aunt's bungalow, and which I was unable to put anywhere else in the time available. I got little for it, but I needed the cash.

This time, on my return to Athens, I was faced with a different method of getting to Stargos. Wishing to avoid my previous reckless reliance on the bus station, Sofia had arranged for me a place in a taxi, crammed in the back with 2 other ladies. It turned out that, by sharing the fare among four people, this way of getting to the port was no more expensive, and a good deal faster, than getting the bus. And of course if one's flight arrived at such a time that getting the early morning bus was impossible without a night's stay in Athens, the logic of taxi transport was paramount.

So, only a few days after my rush to Edinburgh, I was back in Stargos, on the run up to the Easter break. By now, the pace was beginning to hot up for the older, exam classes, and I (now trusted with the keys on my own) had to come in to do sessions with them on Saturday mornings, one of the few days when Sofia was not working long hours. At least there was no one trying for the Cambridge Certificate, which is very difficult. My Greek teacher, Thassoula, had asked me to help her study for this examination, but we found it slow work, the interpretation passages testing all my subtle understanding of English. Indeed I would find when I was preparing that some of the recommended answers disagreed with my reading of the text, which discomfited me. Was an English degree a hindrance here?

Determined to liven up my social life, Thassoula invited me out on some of her late night clubbing sessions, using the flat in town because I could not drive up the hill after the tequila. Thassoula began gently, training me, for I could not cotton on to the habit of setting off for an outing just about when I would be thinking of going home, in the UK. So, the first time, we met at 10.30pm, next time at midnight, the next time at 1 am (well really!) Singularly boring it was, just standing around, posing and drinking. I am a 'doer', not content if not dancing or playing a game, but I knew none of the dances, which looked an impossibly complex blur of feet, as the arm-linked ring revolved. And then there were the leering old gits, beaming unwelcome stares across the room. It really was quite uncomfortable. However, although I was desperately trying to look as if I was not flirting with most of the men there, there was one guy with whom I decided to try out some (limited) language skills. It was at this moment that I realised for the first time the joy of negotiating with the opposite sex in a foreign language. It was not so awkward and embarrassing to say what one meant. Now I am a direct sort of girl, but somehow I could not bear to say to any English-speaking man, 'You are very handsome.' But I was quite happy to blurt out to the gorgeous fireman to whom I was being introduced, *'Poli orios eisai!'* He had the perfect get-out line however (reported through Thassoula). 'When I have learned some English I will get back to you.'

Only twice, not with Thassoula, did I have a better time, when Diane from the WI, married but 'off the leash' it seemed, went to clubs with me, and I was able to dance. I did discover on these occasions that my backside when dancing was a source of fascination for the (Greek) male of the species (and there was me thinking my 'behoochie' was an unattractive encumbrance.) On one occasion, the tables were turned, for I was horribly fascinated to witness the island's most outrageous gay guy ('the best arse in Stargos') gyrating on the dance floor and teasingly dropping his leather trousers to reveal a fetching thong. Oh my, I must have been a little inebriated, for I was moved to pat his backside.

This would no doubt be construed as outrageous behaviour for a female, whose normal job is to remain aloof or manufacture an array of flirtatious glances and gestures. Direct physical action overturned convention. I was soon to discover that this guy had the running of one of the most popular kiosks (*periptero*) on the seafront in Stargos. I thought nothing in particular of this until in later years I heard that kiosks are usually awarded to people who are disabled in some way, for their livelihood. Well I could hardly imagine that this young man's gayness was considered a disability. Maybe it was a family inheritance scenario.

On a more respectable note, there was the gardening club, in which I kept up Elsie's interest. This was useful not only for picking up tips on Mediterranean gardening but also for visiting some of the large villas along the coast, mainly German-owned. My attempts to offer suggestions to people were pretty irrelevant, for, though I had had a large garden in the UK, it was with temperate-loving plants that I had my experience. Though I have since met, for example, aubretia and honeysuckle in Greece, they must be succeeding despite the heat. One great surprise was how well roses do in Greece. We think of them as such an 'English' flower, but they have proved themselves very adaptable to quite another climate.

The weather was gorgeous for the 'WI' trip to the island's greatest beach, on 'kite-flying day' in March. This carnival tradition enlivens the run-up to Lent and is a treat for the children as well as the assisting adults, occasioning picnics and barbeques aplenty. Well the sun may have been shining warmly, but my foolhardy decision to go in swimming was soon regretted. Determined to prove I was a tough Scot, I gritted my teeth, smiled and waved, while slowly turning into a purplish ice block. I had forgotten, or not yet realised, that the water in this area in early Spring is full of the snow-melt from the mainland mountains and not to be attempted by any except the mad or inexperienced before mid May. Somehow surviving, I was well ready to do justice to the excellent picnic, to which all contributed, I producing some sausages cooked on the wood-burning stove.

During this meal, I got talking to Heather, a wonderful Glaswegian, a feisty woman after my own heart. She was the one Elsie had told me ran a dog sanctuary for strays, where I could find access to a reliable vet. Heather shocked me by telling me about the (to us) inexplicably mean attitude of the Greeks in general to this facility. For example, there had been a forest fire in her area (an all too common occurrence in Greece, with Stargos a frequent sufferer.) Despite the fact there could have been many culprits, leaving aside the sun on a broken bottle, Heather's dog sanctuary, and Heather herself, were instantly blamed by the Greek community. It is a sad fact, and foreigners wanting to improve things in Greece should be aware of it, that, while the Greeks may be doing nothing about an issue, eg stray dogs, and have no apparent interest or impetus to do anything, as soon as an outsider does something, they deeply resent it. So the Greeks seem a friendly and welcoming race, until their xenophobia is awakened by a situation like this. One would think they would be glad of someone willing to take action, saving them the trouble. I suppose, in Heather's case, pointing up the humanitarian vacuum in the community would be taken as criticism. Maybe other nations, the British included, would react the same way to foreigners taking the initiative over a social problem, but the issues would never be the same.

Heather had an interesting view of why we various ex-pats had ended up living in another country. She said it was because we were all misfits in our own society. Now one could take that as an insult. Or one could take it that we were not prepared to settle down for the conventional life, but had the courage and the adventure to go and find something more interesting or exciting elsewhere. Certainly, in my case, I always do better when I am allowed a bit of freedom in my work to be creative. (I was first told by that headmaster who betrayed me that I should be 'very creative' with my class. But, when I threw myself into it, he told me I was being 'too creative'.) That was the trouble. I was very creative, which was my driving force, and not just adaptable to change, but wedded to it. I was an individual who liked to stand out, but without the confidence to be a leader. So this misfit (as most do) sacrificed security and a good income to find my way to what was right for me.

I was getting accustomed to going around on my own, so I decided to undertake a longer trip, to the island of Evvia, which lay at the end of the hydrofoil route which went from Stargos and its sister islands, through the port for Athens. Evvia, the third largest island in Greece after Crete and Rhodes, is only just an island, separated as it is from the mainland by a narrow strait. There is a long 'sea loch' behind it at the head of which lies the port which was my destination.

Hydrofoils, in those days, in that area, were a most exciting form of transport, for one could find some space to sit out the back. Probably health and safety rules now forbid this - a shame, for although one could get seriously wet, the sheer excitement of sitting up there zooming along with the glorious foaming wake spraying out behind always gave me a thrill. (I think there is something a bit 'Freudian' going on here) Perhaps a similar sort of excitement was going on in the young man, the *kamaki,* whom I described in the last chapter, who posed for me and stared at me throughout the trip while I remained fascinated but impassive behind my big shades (jolly useful those). As we know, I derived further amusement from seeing him waiting for me by the bus, only to be disappointed.

On reaching Evvia, and acquiring a suitable map, I resolved to walk up the mountain road in order to visit a Monastery. Actually I would normally have called it a convent, as it was for nuns, but in Greece the term monastery seems to cover everything, even things the British would just call churches or chapels. This can cause a few misconceptions, as visitors to Greece often expect to see monks, or hear that monks stayed, at places which were never intended as holy residences. The road was steep but very attractive, though amazingly quiet, hardly a vehicle passing me up or down. This did not worry me at first, until I met some rather numerous, and not necessarily friendly, residents of the island. I realised that, criss-crossing the road I was about to travel were whizzing a great many bees, whose hives scattered the fields on either side. I am not keen on flying insects, which seem to have the knack of buzzing in my ear when I least expect it and startling me - it's the startling I am afraid of. And of course, these ones had stings attached. Although my shoulder-length hair was tied up in a low bun, I patted it nervously.

Well, it was go on or give up, so I marched smartly through, feeling like a moving target in a shooting gallery, acutely aware and nervous of running the gauntlet of hundreds of tiny 'bullets'. Amazingly, the bees missed me completely, and I continued on my way. Sadly the monastery was closed to visitors, so it was not long before I was returning down the steep road. And with a classic, doomed, *hubris* assumed that the bees would miss me again. Not so, for one poor little creature got tangled in my hair and stung my neck. It was at this point that fear washed through me. I had never been stung by a bee before. Wasps yes, totally different chemically. The horror of collapsing with anaphylactic, shock, and lapsing into a fatal coma before I could summon assistance, churned my stomach and tightened my throat. Thank goodness I had never at that time heard of the lore that foretells that if one bee stings a person, as it dies it sends a chemical message to the others who then home in for the attack. On this occasion at least I unwittingly disproved that theory. These were the days before I had a mobile phone. And who could I call anyway? Sofia it would have been. At least she knew where I was going for my trip, but, by the time she could have organised assistance second-hand, it would have been too late. I just had to hope I was not allergic, and as the minutes passed, my nerves, and even the pain, subsided. I was left only with a tiny scab and a lingering guilt that I had caused the death of one of my favourite creatures, the amazing honey bee.

In the early Spring, I discovered the tennis club, a

great social centre, where courses were available from the local pro. Well I had never been much cop at tennis, but my instruction had never been much cop either, so I decided it was worth a try. Over drinks one day at the club, I met Sarah, a very sporty type, and an entertaining companion, who turned out to have an English-teaching qualification which she had never used. Sarah was lithe and athletic but also very well-endowed, no doubt causing heart palpitations in the pro as she bounced her way round the tennis court. Sarah was also local representative for a small travel company which offered villa holidays on Stargos and the neighbouring islands. I had noticed that a lot of the women I met at the 'WI', whether German, Dutch, British or whatever, seemed to work as travel 'reps' in the summer season. A seed was sown in my mind. I had always been good with the public, in my vacation employment and my work in libraries before my teaching days, and I have always been a good organiser. Here might be a chance to stay in Greece over the Summer. The teaching job on Stargos was, after all, only a maternity leave cover, and the long term future for me uncertain.

CHAPTER 8 - ESTATE LIVING

The car had opened up my life on the island, allowing me to travel easily, not beset by bus timetables, all over the island. Another boon, but also a necessity, was the ease with which the shopping could be managed, especially with the tendency for it to rain heavily and relentlessly. Of course, while working at the school, I only had so much time to spend so I resolved to save some of the longer expeditions for when the family came at Easter, when I would have a week off.

But of course I did not just have work at the school now. I had to get used to life and work at the *kalivia* as well. My first priorities were to get to grips with the wood-burning stoves, and to tackle making the animal food. I had always been used to an open fire in Yorkshire, so I had no problems with the principle of lighting a fire and keeping it lit. Indeed, both for joy and necessity, I was soon running the stove in my bedroom as well, so I could have both warmth at bedtime and a delicious slow-cooked stew for next day. My favourite recipe was my own take on the chicken with lemon dish I had come across in restaurants. And I sort of invented my own version of *spetsofai,* the sausage and peppers and tomato casserole, which I did not realise yet was an actual Greek dish. Although I was very fond of Greek sausages (*loukaniko*) with their strong flavour reminiscent of salami, sadly my digestion was not so fond of them, so they became a lunch rather than a dinner treat. I was not much of a fish eater as yet, and would never have attempted to home-cook the squid (*kalamari*) I favoured.

These stoves were messy things to deal with, the 2 main ones each having a firebox 20 cm across by 30 tall, and 45 deep, with a large pan for the fine wood ash below. Any operation produced lots of dust, and the hearth was always needing sweeping. It was a fine art inserting a log into the box, but immensely satisfying to get a good blaze going. I just loved playing with them, and, if I was not closing the outer firebox door to let the oven get hotter, would sit fascinated by their glow, and loving the constantly hot kettle on top, always to hand. And of course on top of the hot stove I could make lentils in soup or bolognaise, and ratatouille, and rice or pasta, all the staples of my accustomed routine for inexpensive re-heatable dishes.

However, the animal food was something to be made in a huge cauldron, on the gas burners of the outside kitchen. Well, it all looked pretty strange to me, assembling dog macaroni, bones from the butcher, *horta,* lemons and garlic and boiling it all up together. I worried a bit about the cats, for I know that they require certain special nutrients (eg taurine for their eyes) which makes cat food more expensive than dog food. But I have to say Charlie and Anna looked the picture of health on their unusual diet. Very likely, they were catching a few mice and such as well, upping their protein ration. I ceased to worry about it. Dishing out the food was a bit of an art too, for as Elsie warned me, if I put all the bowls down together, Nelly would quickly bolt hers and then bully the cats off their dishes and scoff theirs too. So a frustrated Nelly had to be tied up till the cats had had a good go at the dishes, before a tan thunderbolt charged in to hoover up the rest.

I had observed that Nelly was a bit tubby, and indeed Elsie confessed that she never took her for walks. This was why the goat bell had been employed, so that Elsie could let Nelly go off by herself for some exercise, and still be located (even if reluctant to come home, as I discovered.) I resolved to change the routine, and allowed Nelly to roam about in the morning, then tied her up when I went to work, with the promise of a nice long walk in the evening when I got back. I took the risk of removing the goat bell, because I was pretty sure it was driving her crazy, just as I did me. Although never a 'dog' person before, I began to be 'clued in' to the secret of a dog's appeal. Not nearly so mercenary as a cat, a dog exuded friendship and appreciation of what was being done to please it. It was truly a joy to experience the enthusiastic welcome Nelly gave me when I returned from work in the evening. I could see her bouncing about on the end of her rope tie, in the lights of the little car, as I bumped my way along the last of the dirt track.

Because she was so excited, I did not make her wait, but took her for her walk immediately, usually along the track as it went on past the estate, becoming a cliff path leading to the headland at one end of the bay with that beach I had sought at our first meeting. Nelly came to know this routine so well that she would automatically set off that way, and looked almost put out if I fancied going somewhere else for a change, such as uphill towards and through the olive grove. Occasionally, on our walks, we would be followed by one or other of the cats, who unfortunately did not quite get the idea, and would usually rather tryingly campaign to be carried back. I had to be firm about this.

'For goodness sake, Charlie. Are you sure you want to come?' I would cry 'I'm not going to help you get back you know!'

Charlie, whose conversational skills were necessarily limited, would course ignore this advice and be a nuisance as usual. But Nelly thrived on it, becoming a rather fitter dog than I had inherited. The night walks only had one down side, the dogs on guard with the herd of goats, which was kept at night in pens on the opposite slope of the adjoining valley. They, of course, would sense Nelly's presence as a dog on the loose, albeit from quite a distance away, and make a bit of a racket, somewhat spoiling the relaxing peace of the activity.

Walks were not the only way that I spoiled Nelly. Of a cold evening, when I was ensconced in front of the stove, music playing, getting on with sewing cushion covers or reading, I had not the heart to leave Nelly tied up outside as Elsie had instructed. Later, I came to learn that this was the Greek way with dogs, certainly in rural areas, the toy lapdogs of Athens being an exception. Now I might have been able to conceal this defiance of instructions, except that I had done some drawings of the animals, in which it was quite obvious that Nelly was lying on the living room sofa; bit of a give-away. Elsie, when she saw it and realised, was good-natured about it, luckily.

Nelly

When feeding the chickens, one had to have a long stick at the ready, for the rooster was rather aggressive. Opening the gate, carrying the corn and fending him off was a bit tricky with only two hands. I realised I would have to carry the corn in a bag over my arm, not the bowl Elsie used. It made me wonder if Elsie ever even bothered to go into the enclosure to look for eggs. Mind you, I never found any eggs in the early part of my stay. The hens, (but strangely not the rooster) escaped on a regular basis. It was tiresome to have to chase them back down the hill and open the gate. I soon discovered that if I just left them alone, keeping them out of the rooms of course, they would find their way back into the enclosure. I made a few early efforts to identify holes in the hedge and try to fill them with branches, but to no avail. I still had loose hens and loose hen poop around the place. I would have to 'up my game' here, it seemed.

I found that there was other animal life around beyond the domestic ones. It was quite amusing, however, following my initial reaction to the regular beeping noise in the night (assumed to be someone's irritating car alarm) when I discovered that it was in fact the call of the impossibly cute little Skops owl - whereupon, because it was natural, the noise stopped bothering me altogether. But if I liked the owls, I found my favourites to be the geckos. These little chaps, consumers of mosquitoes (hurray!) inhabited mainly the bathroom, and came out to hunt when there was no one around. I was sorry they were so shy, for their squeaky cries and 'playdoh' physiques I found very appealing. So I conceived a way of catching them out. I would sneak up to the bathroom door very quietly, and then suddenly enter the room, switching on the light simultaneously. Caught out in the open, the geckos, 5 or 6 of various sizes, would squeak and make a dash for the nearest gap behind the panelling.

Having a shower in that bathroom was not for the faint-hearted. First, one had to make sure the water heater *(thermosyphono)*had been on for a sufficient time, but also that one had put the wall heater on to raise the temperature sufficiently above frigid to summon up the courage to disrobe. Scot or not, I was still used to central heating inside the house, even if the east winds of Edinburgh and the snows of Yorkshire had built a certain weather resistance. My Scottish friend gave me such a laugh when she told me of her boyfriend, observing her spraying on deodorant, laconically remarking, 'Another Scottish shower, May?'

The lemon tree needed no attention, and I just luxuriated in the joy of having the fresh picked fruit sliced in a hot morning cup. I even showed Elsie this before she left, to have it pronounced 'delicious'. It did make me wonder, this inability of Elsie after all these years to make the best use of all the bounty of her own estate.

The vineyard was to wait for Elsie's return before any activity took place, and I did not even have to weed among the vines, for it was here that the precious '*horta*' grew, a leaf similar to dandelion but sharing some of the succulent qualities of spinach. Doused with olive oil and lemon, it was a Greek winter favourite soon to be one of mine too. However, this popularity had its down side, for the locals at the *kalivia* had not been slow to spot Elsie's vineyard's potential as a prime *horta*-hunting spot. More than once, I was startled on my return from work to find a couple of Greek ladies or gents, bent double, knifing their way round the vineyard in search of the iron-rich green harvest. Well, what a cheek! I thought, inclined to be 'feisty Fran' when it came to defending my rights or territory. But I held off challenging the interlopers, for a number of reasons. Firstly, I did not know for sure if this was custom and practice between Elsie and her neighbours. Secondly, if it were not, I had no wish to queer the pitch for Elsie. And thirdly, there was enough *horta* to go round. Still, it would have been nice to be consulted on a 'by your leave'

One way I learned to get on with the Greeks was by offering lifts into town for anyone I passed at the bus stop. This was met with fulsome gratitude and (presumably) 'brownie points' for being a decent sort. After all, if anything went wrong, the neighbours would need to be called on for assistance, as with the English neighbour at the time of my aunt's death.

The most arduous task I had was the storing of the winter log supply. This, I found to my alarm on returning one late January day, was simply tipped over the back gate by the delivery man, so the yard was strewn with a 3-foot-high pile. Somehow, I found space in the bins (cunningly built in as bench seats round the patios) for most of it, while the rest could be brought into the rooms in readiness for use. Hmm, I thought, I never saw myself reinvented as a lumberjack. But I amused myself with renditions of the 'Lumberjack Song' from Monty Python while bending my increasingly aching back to the seemingly endless task.

Even though I was pretty conserving of gas, there came the moment when the bottle of petro-gas in the outside kitchen ran out. A feeling of doom hung over me. But I had been given instructions what to do, down to where to take the used bottle. In the event, nervous though I was, changing the bottle was relatively easy. What could have gone wrong for that poor woman who was burnt to death? When I mentioned this to Sofia, she told me that sometimes people put a flame to the nozzle of a gas bottle to check if it is really empty. What madness was this? Yes, the equivalent in terms of the 'Darwin Awards' to a UK person hunting for a gas leak with a lighted match in hand. Having discovered that stupidity had been the major factor, I was far less nervous of changing the bottle in the indoor kitchen when the time came.

So I had plenty of day-to-day life occurrences to record in the 'sit rep' as Elsie called it, which I sent her on a regular basis. And she would write to me, the first letter being an account of her arrival in London, and a few more tips about the estate and Stargos life in general. In the first case, her method to provide support for the peas 'is to stick in twiggy bits at judicious intervals', she reminded me about a new tree she had planted which needed watering, and expressed wonder that I had managed to wash the rug. In the second case, for example, I was told of a good hairdresser, and how to handle a crisis requiring a vet. I had noticed Charlie limping and, fearful of neglecting an animal not belonging to me, went to the vet in town, which cost 3,000 drachmas (about £6) for not much help. Although Elsie agreed to pay for the visit, she said that vet was useless and I should leave the animals to get over minor things by themselves. For anything major, I should call Heather from the dog sanctuary who had regular visits from a vet from the neighbouring island.

But beyond the necessities of daily living, the opportunities for creative 'wombling' were opened up. My attraction to life at the *Kalivia* had been largely based on the challenge to my creativity laid down by Elsie's invitation to improve things as I found I could. So began an amusing time when I scouted around for cast-off items which would contribute to the household.

CHAPTER 9 - WONDERS OF CREATION

In my searches for useful free materials for creative recycling, one fertile hunting ground was the carpenter's workshop, which usually had surplus bits and pieces outside, up for grabs eg a section of log, wooden cupboard doors, and, most usefully, 2 glass doors with glass intact. So, what could 'wombling Fran' do with these? As the far area of the patio was a bit lacking in furniture, I decided that the log could be the base, and the one of the cupboard doors (about 3 feet long) could be the top, for a new coffee table. But there was the other door. I managed to find a wooden crate to support that: so, two coffee tables. The glass doors had immediately suggested themselves as material for a cold frame for the seedlings. I needed to build up the sides with bits of brick and paving stone, making sure to achieve a slight slope for the rain. Opening and closing the frame was a bit tricky, with no hinges, but one half could be slid on top of the other. Well, I was totally proud of myself, but could not really tell anyone, until I got to the gardening club.

Sofia tended to go a bit quiet and scowling if I mentioned activities at Elsie's, so I had learned not to share my enthusiasms there. But she could not fault me at work. She also needed my help with something, and I was glad to be able to give something back after so many favours from her. It was all a bit puzzling to me, this, but it seemed that some people who had a house had asked Sofia to watch over it in the Winter. They also had a jeep, which needed some work doing on it. The only trouble was, Sofia was unable to drive the jeep to the garage because she had the wrong sort of licence, meaning she could not drive a car with a gearshift. Here was another challenge, and though I was nervous, I soon got to grips with the jeep's controls, and followed Sofia on her bike as we made our way across town to the garage. Then she gave me a lift on her bike back to the Yugo. That was the only time I was ever on Sofia's bike, which normally just had room for her and loads of books to mark. I am not good on a motorbike, and two well-built ladies tested its powers of locomotion to the limit. Well, I could not complain that we went too fast, anyway.

My eccentricity was confirmed, for the residents of the town, when I was seen making off with the wooden frame on which a washing machine had been stood in its packing. This was destined to be the frame for the back piece needed by Elsie's bench outside the living room. It had to be covered with other wood, and for this I collected driftwood on the nearby beach - that beach which I had found too hard to find on my first, historic, expedition to the area. It certainly was a steep path, and very narrow, deeply cleft between banks and edged with overhanging scrubby bushes. The ground was slippery, sandy soil, with patches of scree, sudden sharp ascents, and unexpected potholes. In other words, not too great to negotiate when carrying 'finds' on one's back. One of the most awkward (but rewarding) was the (perfect) purple plastic chair, which I presume must have fallen off a boat. Still, it was not heavy, like the driftwood, or unwieldy, like the canes, which were also long and scratchy. However, there was an enormous satisfaction from using these canes which I not had to pay the garden centre for. Now I had a cold frame for the runner bean seedlings and their eventual climbing frame. I had also further improved the furniture on the patio.

Previously, I had taken up hand sewing in the evening, while listening to music. It's wonderful what one can find to do when not distracted by the television. So gradually a series of cushions started brightening up Elsie's living room, stuffed with either her worn out cushions or with foam from the big bag I had bought. Because I had bought a large array of different sized remnants from the fabric shop at the end of the main street, I was also able to make-to-measure cushions that would fit the outside bench to which I was making additions. Joining in with the 'WI' project to make a large quilt from sewing together squares designed and made by different members, I had a lot of fun putting on appliqué butterflies and reminding myself how to do blanket stitch to do it.

One rather eccentric ambition in the art and craft line for which I bought some equipment I never actually got round to trying out. I had been studying the top of the door at Elsie's living room, and decided there would be a way to suspend a row of 'warp' threads, weighted with large bolts (which I acquired) so that a rug could be woven. Maybe it would have worked. I need to get a carpenter to make me a frame, and realise the rug-making ambition (though secretly I would enjoy it more if I had invented my own 'Heath Robinson' technology to do it.)

One great irritation was the way the planks on top of the water butts kept falling in to the water. I (no expert with wood) could hardly believe that Elsie had been so feckless as not to use my own simple solution of assembling the planks into 2 halves and nailing 2 battens across underneath each half, to make a 2-part lid. They were a little short for the space, but with careful balancing they worked fine.

It was clear to me that Elsie had not cleaned the outside kitchen for a very long time. Motivated by the need to impress with my industry, by the desire to have cleaner surroundings to work in, and by the urge to have the place looking good for holiday time, I set about remedying this. During this messy task, I came across an item in the corner which Elsie had mentioned to me - a mysterious brown object, like a small coconut, which Elsie had found and kept aside in a blue plastic beaker. Unfortunately, having studied it, and put it back, I forgot about it again, which was to lead to one of the saddest and most poignant incidents of my stay at the *kalivia*. One night a few weeks later, out in the kitchen, I heard a strange soft scratching noise coming from the corner. On investigation, I found the blue plastic beaker, now occupied not by what had obviously been a cocoon, but by a HUGE moth, far too big for the space it was trapped in.

Now I am terrified of moths, with their unerring tendency to flutter to the back of my neck and startle me, but my heart went out to this poor creature. It had hatched out, but had not had enough space in which to expand its magnificent wings. Gingerly, horribly fascinated, I managed to tip the struggling insect out of the beaker. It was worse than I thought. One wing was not too bad, but the other was just a shrivelled strip. There would be no mating flight for this amazing creature, a giant hawk moth. I realised how vulnerable the poor thing would be to the cats, but somehow I could not bring myself to kill it. I hid it on a bush by the back gate, hoping the cats would decide they were now in for the night and not disturb it.

Anxiously, I rushed out the next morning to see if the moth was still there, and was rewarded with an amazing sight. It seemed there was a God after all, for there, sitting on the bush, was indeed the crippled moth, but next to it, with one of its wings over-lapping, was another giant hawk-moth. This beautiful, perfect creature had found its fellow and appeared to be comforting it. No doubt it was the astonishing pheromones these creatures exude which had attracted it. Was this a male attempting to mate with a stricken female? Did they succeed, and did anything come of the union? I stood, awestruck, tears welling up, but had to drag myself away, inwardly cursing that I had no film in the camera. What a tale I would have to tell Elsie now! Already, I felt guilty for over-looking the cocoon till too late, and causing the moth to be damaged. But now there was this bitter-sweet scene to contemplate - and of course 2 moths at the mercy of the cats. I had to drag myself away to go to work, but was a bit preoccupied during the lessons. However, when I returned home, both of the moths had gone. I simply had to steel myself not to brood too much on the likely end of their story.

Once the good weather looked settled, in late February, early March, I took on the back-breaking task was of washing the blankets, by hand. I had always prided myself on being strong, but I nearly over-reached myself with this job. On reflection, there was probably no need to do this task (despite the hovering question of when, if ever, the blankets had been washed in years.) But I was keen to make the place nice and fresh for the family coming on holiday. Sadly, one casualty of the job was the wedding ring I had inherited from my grandmother, worn ornamentally, but foolishly left on during the blanket dunking. Next thing I knew, my finger was empty and the ring un-findable (except presumably by the metal detector which I jokingly suggested to Elsie later) So, there's gold in them thar hills' took on a new meaning in Stargos.

As the weather warmed up, other factors about Greek country living asserted themselves. I have never been diligent about doing washing up promptly, for it is a job I hate, and I would rather save up the dishes and have one big (albeit dreary) session. Well, once the ants started to emerge, I soon learned what neglected plates and food waste could mean, and smartened up my act. If ever really pushed for time, I learned to rinse the plates quickly then leave them upside down in the washing up bowl, which deterred the ants.

Although I liked the noise of the geckos, and got used to the regular almost electronic beep of the Skops owl, the bees were another thing, and I had to find a way to mask the apparently ominous buzzing as the insects swarmed around the fruit blossom just outside the living room. Very loud music helped, though there was always that extra 'backing track'. It was quite a relief when the sun went down and the bees retired for the night. Another great delight was to watch the beautiful herd of goats come past the back gate from their night time pens in the valley above the beach, down the road

to further pasture. The bells gave advance warning of their approach, and soon a stream of tan and cream and black and white clattered past, with the goatherd on his donkey, and his two dogs, in attendance.

Getting used to, and getting to love, life on the estate naturally made me hanker after my own place, which I could set up and run just as I wished. Following the death of my aunt, it occurred to me that I was going to have some money coming to me, so I decided to try looking at some property. Greek teacher Thassoula said she knew a guy who had a house to sell in the hills, so, trustingly, I agreed to meet him. He, Michalis, spoke English quite well, but was a wild-haired, bearded, hippy- looking type, with a crippled leg (from polio in childhood), his age hard to determine but probably early 30s.

It was a Sunday afternoon, quite sunny, when Michalis and I set off in the little Yugo (which already had one cracked suspension strut, in need of attention). Out of town, the roads of Stargos fall into 2 main types - the main perimeter which is well-surfaced with tarmac, and the dirt-track type. These roads last cut through the woods, often up quite steep slopes. And Stargos is heavily wooded, mostly with wonderful Mediterranean conifers, and more so at the Western end. There is little in between (the concrete hill to the *kalivia* being an exception here). It was with some alarm (knowing the deficiencies of the car) that I studied the first of the dirt-track roads I was going to have to negotiate. But, never one to give up, I ventured forth. There then ensued 3 hours of nail-biting rally driving, challenged by roads deeply gouged by heavy winter rains.

'I can't get the car across there!' I exclaimed, confronted with a particularly deep trough.

'Don't worry, I get out and fix something!' offered Michalis.

It was almost farcical, the performance of this poor crippled guy continually having to get out of the car to build little causeways of stones, branches etc for me to drive gingerly across. Somewhere in the midst of this seemingly endless ordeal, we stopped on a hillside and looked across a valley to see the house in question.

'Why can't we get any closer?' I enquired.

'Um, there is not road…' admitted Michalis.

It seemed to me obvious that there must be a road (though it was probably worse than those we had up to now traversed) but that Michalis was using this as an excuse to prevent me from seeing the place any closer. Even at a distance, it looked half fallen down, and its situation deep in a gloomy valley added nothing to whatever appeal he had imagined it might have. Needless to say, the rest of the journey was a grim affair, both of us exhausted, and I rather annoyed to have had my time wasted on such a hopeless prospect. Nevertheless, we stopped in the dusk of the seafront to have a coffee, which I managed to consume in politeness, though vowing privately that I never wanted to see this misguided chap again.

Here was another learning experience, to find that Greeks would often assume that foreigners were (a) loaded and (b) devoid of commonsense. It beggared belief that Michalis had expected me to take the whole premise seriously. The only good thing which came out of the expedition was that, so relieved was I that the 'off road rally' experience had not wiped out the little car completely, that I decided to stop living on borrowed time and get the suspension fixed forthwith.

But I had not lost the urge to find my own place in Greece. I discovered an estate agency which was advertising a little house in the back streets, which had a small yard, and also a most attractive asset: a two-storey barn in the yard, ripe for conversion to studio, apartments, whatever. Here, I thought, I could have my own art studio, even a pottery, and develop the upstairs into guest apartments. It had to be said that the main house, reminiscent of a small prefab bungalow in appearance, layout and space, was no great shakes, but the land and the barn made it an attractive prospect for development. Land, in that area of Stargos town, was a rare commodity, as the terrain was mostly quite sloping, and houses were built right onto the street, with a small courtyard at most in the 'territory'. However, there were other people interested in the property. I was forced to admit that the money from my inheritance was unlikely to be forthcoming in the near future, so, while still expressing my interest, I had to stand by and see my potential haven of creativity be sold to someone else.

CHAPTER 10 - HOLIDAY TIME

At Carnival time, just before Lent, my flamboyant streak was allowed full rein at when there was a party at the school which involved dressing up. The kids, arrayed in their costumes, were slightly bemused at the sight of me, got up as a 'big cat', complete with leopard skin leggings (part of my pyjamas), tiger ears and tail (a most awkward 3 foot long item, heavily wired swinging from my waistband.) I decided that this attempt to show what a good sport and (literally) 'party animal' I was had fallen a bit flat, and made me more of a figure of embarrassment than someone deserving of respect. Maybe in a Greek community it is less acceptable for fun-loving adults to join in with the kids. Is there is a demarcation? Silly behaviour is for children, but dignity for adults. Well I can think of a few men who throw fireworks at Easter, on whom that demarcation is lost.

Elsie had been clear that once I was ensconced at the estate, I could invite what visitors I liked, as had others before. So my father, (let's call him Dad) just turned 80 but very fit, and my sons, Thomas soon to be 19, and James coming up 17, decided to make the trip for a couple of weeks in the

Easter holidays, beginning in late March in the UK. It would be essential to get the car fixed, for the family coming. Not only was the suspension known to be cracked, but the brakes definitely needed attention. What had held me back, really, was the feeling that Elsie would somehow blame me for what had been an existing problem, and, even if she did not, would be reluctant to pay for the repair. As it turned out, she agreed that I should go ahead and would be reimbursed, because it seemed that the guy who had sold her the car not long before had been supposed to fix both of these repairs before handing it over. I accepted that if a problem was day to day stuff - eg a puncture, I would be liable for the cost. This seemed fair enough, for the little car was such a boon.

I had worked hard on general cleaning and estate improvements, but now it was time to create something else; suitable sleeping accommodation for my men-folk. I reckoned that my father would be fine in the inner bedroom of the right hand wing. Over there, there was a second toilet, and a small kitchen. Elsie's own room was at the end of the base of the 'L' and we left that untouched. I began by investigating the workings of the stove, for I would only make a mess doing that. This was yet another different type, a small cast iron one with an upright chimney and no oven. It was a lovely and quite large room, opening off the South East facing patio, with a small window at the back. The bed was quite big, a typical slatted pine affair, but with plenty of the (newly-washed!) blankets, and the stove on the go, Dad should be quite comfortable.

With the boys, I was not so sure. The only remaining sleeping quarters were in what had once been the garage, at the entrance of the estate. This had twin beds, a small chest of drawers and not much else, apart from a side window and the inevitable stove - of yet another type. This one had a chimney which bent 90 degrees and traversed the ceiling to vent at the side. Now, having these crossing chimneys is a mixed blessing. Firstly, if they have bends and joints, they can leak. But at the same time, they get very hot, and can therefore add to the distribution of heat in the room. Then, of course, one has to be careful not to accidentally brush against the pipe, for fear of scorches. As it happened, the testing of the stove did not go that well, and I was in two minds whether to use it, as it seemed not worth the trouble for such poor function. At least I had an electric heater about the place as back up. And this would be the coldest room, having the thinnest walls, and no protection from enclosing buildings. But hey, boys are tough.

I went to Athens to meet them. Dad, nearly 6 feet, silver-haired, blue-eyed, very hale for his near-80 years, smart in blazer and flannels, was flanked by Thomas and James. Both are tall, with James the taller at just over 6 feet. Thomas is darker-haired, and both have their father's wonderful expressive eyebrows, and my blue/green eyes. Altogether a handsome crew to welcome aboard the good ship Elsie. The bus trip from Athens, which normally displayed some lovely scenery, was marred by lots of fog en route, not a promising sign. Indeed, as can happen in Greek Springs, the weather went colder than it had been in mid-February. Nevertheless, the novelty of it all entranced the family. As I had hoped, Dad was thrilled with his room, which became quite cosy with the stove. The 'garage' room the boys had was chilliest and required the one electric heater at night. Following my first, unsatisfactory, experiment with the stove in there, things got worse, and the place filled with fumes from the long chimney across the ceiling, which was leaking. Thank goodness this did not happen at night when they were asleep.

I was still working for the first week, so that had to be planned round, with me dropping the family in town for a rendezvous later, or coming back up the hill to pick them up. As anyone who has lived with teenage children will avow, mornings are a rather sketchy concept for them when not required to trudge off to school, so my chances of achieving joint activity before going to work were curtailed. Thomas (a student of Physics) was much taken with the beach, and would spend several happy hours one afternoon, playing at diverting the little stream which ran onto it. The boys helped me prepare my driftwood pieces, which needed sanding down before being attached to the bench back (that washing machine packing case base. And then there was looking for the eggs, roaming around the over-vast enclosure. This led James to write in the journal, for Elsie's benefit, his simple suggestion that she make the enclosure smaller. The eggs which Thomas eventually found could have been there for any length of time, of course, so we did not dare cook them.

When it came to cooking, one great excitement was to use the outside fireplace, though on one occasion my choice of fish to bake was not a good one, being rather bony – but luckily there were baked potatoes and sausages to compensate. A greater success was the shrimp pasta dish which Sofia's husband Kostas taught me to make. This necessitated my first visit to the fish market to purchase these as well as the less successful bony fish. I was a bit insulted, when at the fish market, by the comments of one of the 'WI' ladies I encountered, that she was going to have to muscle in and help me because I would not know what I was doing. Feisty Fran (a Leo born in the Year of the Tiger) felt her hackles rise at this, but managed at least to be civil - 'I'm fine!'

Of course the car was a major boon in expanding the possibilities of the holiday. However, its use led to a brush with mortality. Out in the car, on the way to a beach during my day off, we were negotiating the narrow steep hill, with difficult camber and rather deep edging ditch which had caused me trouble on my trial drive in December. But we were coming down, and had reached beyond half-way, when a green car passed on the other side, quite safely, to be suddenly and alarmingly followed by a great sparkling flash in the sky, and the appearance 'out of the blue' of a blue car, as if dropped from above (true actually!) slewed diagonally across the narrow road, blocking it completely.

'Bloody hell!' cried mother and sons in unison...

'Yikes!' said Dad

'What the ****!?' I continued, 'Where...uh, uh, what??'

As our astonished family watched open-mouthed, a young man leapt out of the apparition, amazingly unharmed: good heavens, he must have been wearing his seat belt! He proceeded to remove his baseball cap and hurl it to the ground, then started kicking the car accompanied by suitable Greek oaths. Well, it was plain that the family outing was going nowhere, so I got out to offer some assistance. Luckily, the youth spoke English quite well.

'Please, please can you take me to my father?' he pleaded.

'But where?' I enquired.

'Up the hill, that way!' he pointed.

My bemused and slightly shocked family were waiting.

'Sorry guys, why not get out and sit on the side while I see what I can do?

'We can't go anywhere for a while anyway.' said Thomas

'Well, it's nice of you to help him, Mum,' added James.

Despite my lack of Greek, I had already established that I and the young man could communicate, and as we drove he proceeded to explain the reason for his plight. It seemed that this was his mother's car, and he was very anxious to get up the hill to summon his father (as it emerged, hoping to have Dad there before the Police got wind of the accident). I had studied the car, which had little glass left. It did not look too bad on the offside, but a quick look at the nearside produced an involuntary gasp, and a perfect illustration of the term 'mangled'. As he continued to relate what had happened, the reason for his particular nervousness emerged. He was only 16, and had no driving licence, nor, of course, any insurance. On we drove, up past Elsie's estate and along the cliff road.

Crikey, how far is this guy's house? I thought, as we bounced along unfamiliar and questionable roads. It seemed that the lad had been trying to maintain speed so as to deal with the steepness of the hill. (We remember me, on my first attempt, stalling, having lost momentum). He had thus taken the bend too fast – and run into the olive tree at the side of the road at the foot of the hill after the bend. The car had shot skywards and turned over in the air, to appear like 'Tardis' from nowhere some 30 meters in front of my car.

I was torn between incredulity that the lad had emerged unscathed from the crash, and the chill of growing horror, as I realised how close I and my family had come to being killed or seriously injured by this young road hog. Well, we got to the family home at last, but, though reasonably expected thanks from the father, I was rudely disappointed, for I merely got a glower which seemed to imply his putting the blame on me. He rapidly swept his errant offspring into a large 4 wheel drive jeep and roared off, leaving a rather glum Fran to follow, chugging along, back to the family.

Golly, I wonder if the Police will want a statement from me? I was thinking, worried that my Greek was virtually nil, and the Police not noted for their command of English. For indeed, upon my return, the Police were in attendance, summoned by one of the motorists who had been trying to ascend the hill and found his way blocked. Quite a crowd had assembled, observed by my father and sons. Slightly to my disappointment at the time (but ultimately to my relief), the Police were totally uninterested in anything I might have had to say about the accident. Their concern was to roll the car a bit more off the road into the ditch so that at least one lane of traffic could squeeze past. So, happily, after not much more delay, the beach-bound family were soon on our way.

There was a bit of a post-script, and indeed I was agog for news of the outcome. Having related my hair-raising experience to one of my classes, the teenagers explained that the boy in question had been far from contrite over his experience (and lucky escape!). In fact he had been boasting in the cafes about the incident as if it were a daring exploit to be proud of!

'Good grief! My family and I might have been killed!' I exclaimed, shocked. 'What's going to happen? Has he not been punished?'

'Ah,' said young Kostas, 'nothing will happen to him. His mother's car is destroyed, but the Police will do nothing because his father is the Mayor's brother!'

I, ever over-burdened with an exaggerated sense of fairness, and thus often disappointed in human nature and the dealings of those in power, was dismayed that the cocky lad should get off scot-free. Yet I was heartened at the disgust expressed by the teenagers in the school, which proved that at least some young Greeks had decent impulses. And here, of course, was an introduction to the grand old Greek tradition of 'it's not what you know, but who you know', or to put it another way, the power of having a benevolent connection (preferably in the family) inside an important organisation.

The water was pretty cold for swimming still, but the beaches of Stargos are famously wonderful, so a few visits were made. Thus the family were privileged to see these stretches of beautiful sand, backed by pine woods, with not a soul on them but ourselves. James was particularly entranced with the largest of these beaches and sat for ages just drinking in the perspective, and later took lots of photographs. I had been to this famous beach, with the 'WI' back in early March, on 'kite-flying day', which was gloriously sunny. However, my bravado ('I'm a Scot, I can take it!') about entering the water was nearly rewarded with hypothermia.

One must was a visit to the famous 'Banana Beach'. The origins of the name were a bit mysterious, but may (to my rather dirty mind) have been associated with the nature of the

normal occupants of the beach. In the Season, it was the haunt of nudists. I heard a good story about a guy on this beach who braved the water in the buff, despite jellyfish warnings. Well, of course soon there was a scream and he emerged clutching his appendage – a case of being well-stung, not well-hung! At this point, all the other male would-be swimmers retreated from the water's edge and reappeared shortly afterwards in their 'back-up' swimming shorts. Luckily during our rather cold swim we met no jelly-fish. But I did take away a trophy of some unusual driftwood, rather jelly-fish shaped.

During expeditions to the beaches, we had spotted a nice looking taverna, which we decided to visit for dinner. Happily, it turned out to be run by Stavros, husband of a very nice New Zealander, Pat, whom I knew from the 'WI'. It was here that, somewhat to my surprise, my sons cemented a lasting passion for 'taramasalata' that tasty concoction of cod's roe, olive oil and bread. In most eateries, it came out of a catering company's large tub, in a startlingly unnatural pink colour. But in Stavros's place it was home-made, subtle coloured, and fabulously flavoured. It is almost a shame that, ever after, the lads have had to make do with the commercial pink stuff, instead of the wonderful exemplar which first got them interested.

The second week of the family's holiday included Greek Easter, marked in the favourite taverna of Stargos town by the presentation of red dyed hard-boiled eggs. We decided to spend the night of Good Friday in Town, and go to the main church to see the service. However, though entranced by the sight of the crowd standing in the beautiful courtyard all holding candles, were quickly put off by the constant startling bangs of the fireworks which were being thrown by (mainly) small boys. My nerves would not stand the hanging around in all this noise, and the others were bemused anyway, so we all went home. None of us could understand the seeming lack of respect for the solemn occasion, which these fireworks seemed to imply. We had heard that Greek Easter was as important as Christmas in the UK, or more so. So what was going on here? I was later to hear a 'justification' for the fireworks along the lines of the bangs being used to scare away the Devil so he could not prevent the Resurrection.

Despite my efforts to get the Yugo repaired in time for the family's visit, the car had developed another problem, and had to go into the garage. As I had helped Sofia to deliver her friends' jeep, she agreed to let me borrow it to take the family around for a day or two. Though not blessed with a good sense of direction, I am fairly intrepid about the roads I am prepared to tackle. But this time, exploring the mountain tracks after visiting the large Monastery, trying to find a route through to the Kastro and mountain village I struck a ticklish problem. Suddenly, the single track road was blocked off with a sign.

'Mum you'll have to go back!' urged James.

'Nonsense, it'll be all right!' I insisted.

But it wasn't. Round the next bend, we found a huge pile of branches blocking the road.

'Blast!' I cried, 'It's going to be jolly difficult reversing here!'

I put the jeep in reverse, and began the uphill manoeuvre. Not much happened, but a lot of noise, and, alarmingly, a strong smell of burning rubber.

'Christ, I'm burning the clutch out!' I wailed. 'You'll have to get out, the car's too heavy!'

Thankfully, with the three men out of the car, I was able to get it to move, and, after finding a slightly wider spot, to do about an 18-point turn.

'Sorry about that folks! Glad to get out of there...'

'Well, you are resourceful!' said Dad, charmingly.

'Better just go somewhere else then,' suggested Thomas.

And none of them was mean to me over the near disaster – nice guys! As it happened, we found a better route to the Monastery, which we greatly enjoyed, being a large and wonderful building constructed like a typical cloister round a central courtyard. The grounds were lovely, and featured ducks, geese and even swans among the inhabitants.

But we did not always go out in the car, and on more

than one occasion set off to walk along the tracks above the beaches. On one particularly long walk, accompanied, of course, by Nelly (though thankfully not by the cats), the said dog began to flag considerably. Despite her nightly exercise, it seemed Nelly still had some work to do on her fitness and stamina. She certainly thrived on all the attention from the extra inhabitants, as indeed did the cats. We all missed our old family cat, whom I had had since before the boys were born, and who, nearly 21 and with failing health, had to be put down shortly before I came to Greece.

When the rural idyll came to an end for Dad and the boys, I was unable to accompany them to Athens for their return. However, as they knew the drill, or at least capable organiser Thomas now did, I was not anxious about them during their journey. And at least I could be sure of one thing. Unlike me as a single female, this group of guys would be of no appeal to predatory *kamaki* males.

CHAPTER 11 - ELSIE'S ENDGAME

After the family's departure, I concentrated on some final tasks on the estate, leading up to Elsie's return. The boys had helped me with sanding the wood for the bench back, which I duly put together. I tended the seedlings I had raised in the cold frame. I finished the last of the cushion covers, and washed the curtains.

But always hovering annoyingly was the matter of the wretched hens. Their huge enclosure obviously had lots of holes in the fence, given the hens' talent for escaping and pooping all over the patio (and the house if they could get in). I did not have to tackle the local hardware merchants, as Elsie already had a large roll of chicken wire in stock – but, again, had been too lazy, dilatory etc to put it to use. Now, Fearless Fran had not handled chicken wire before, though I had done many messy scratchy jobs in my Yorkshire garden over the years. I was glad there was no one observing my trial and error antics until a suitable method of laying-out and cutting was found.

It is a good job that I have the character of an Amazon, not a 'princess', for I was to get considerably scratched and filthy as I fought the hedge to find the gaps, and then fought again to insert and fasten wire where deemed necessary. But what a reward! At last the hens stopped escaping and began to lay in the right place (encouraged by the ceramic pretend egg). Ironically, I would have felt less aggrieved about the whole business of the hens if I had known then what I know now. Being a 'townie' whose eggs came in supermarket cartons, I did not realise that hens are seasonal layers, unless fed with unnatural hormones to make them produce eggs all year round. So my grumbling about the non-production of eggs by these creatures, who proceeded to eat their heads off and make lots of mess, would have been silenced by a tip-off from Elsie. Maybe it did not occur to her that I simply did not know.

The *frontistirio* year, for me, was effectively nearing an end, as the exams for the pupils I was concerned with were in early May, and I would be a bit supernumerary after that. Sofia esteemed my value as a teacher sufficiently to be concerned with what would happen to me after the maternity leave cover finished. She had started putting out feelers in Naplos on the mainland, familiar to me as the source of my holiday suitcase. Her friend Glenda, a fellow-American, though not Greek American, had contacts there amongst the numerous schools in the city. It was not long before Glenda came up with a *frontistirio* owner who was interested in working with me, and wanted to meet me.

Off I went on the hydrofoil to Naplos, and met Lina, a very attractive and charming young woman, with strikingly beautiful long dark auburn hair. Lina was impressed with my willingness to undertake composition supervision, indeed to involve myself creatively in the general enrichment of the teaching and preparation of materials. She did say that, as she could not give me many hours, she would be asking one or maybe two other small schools if they were interested in employing me (that valuable commodity, a native speaker), to enable me to reach a viable living wage. This sounded sensible, and useful to both sides, so I went along with it. I was to regret my casual acceptance of such a strategy, as things turned out.

So time ticked on till the reappearance of Elsie in late April. As it happened, it was a weekend, without any evening duty for me, but nevertheless Elsie insisted on getting a taxi, so as not to drag me down the hill to hang around for the hydrofoil to arrive. Nelly did not know where to put herself when she saw the beloved figure emerge from the taxi in the evening light, and lope down the hill. I could not suppress a few jealous pangs, as the surrogate mistress soon to be relinquished once more.

I, of course, was very excited about showing Elsie all the things I had been doing. Once she had stowed her stuff, I took her for a tour of the patio, pointing out new furniture, into the garden to see the beans on their frame, and finally to the water butt with its new lid. It was here that I gained the first clue that Elsie was not 100% keen on the improvements made by temporary inhabitants, whatever her positive urgings might have been. With a little 'oops!' and a decidedly naughty twinkle in her eye, she deliberately pushed my new wooden lids into the water-butt. Now I have quite a volatile temper, but I managed to control it and ignore the incident, though not in my own thoughts. I put forward that, now she had come home, I should leave Elsie to enjoy her estate, and return to my flat in town. This was met with an exclamation of

'Please don't go!'

I was somewhat surprised (but a bit flattered I confess) by her request that I stay on at the estate. I had thought to be around only long enough for an explanation and hand over, but I was persuaded to stay on. Well, it was lovely up there. Over the next few days, Elsie was able to see further results of my labours in the cleanliness of the establishment, (in particular the outside kitchen), and the fruitful behaviour of the hens. Elsie managed to make positive noises, and I put down my perception of little suitable praise to my usual over-achiever's lack of satisfaction.

We began together the fascinating task of preparing the vines. This was when I learned of the symbiotic nature of the Greek dish *dolmades* or stuffed vine leaves. For the vines had to be stripped of two thirds of their leaves, which then might as well be put to good use! I let Elsie do the stripping while I followed on to tie them to the wires according to her instructions.

During this time, Elsie surprised me by asking if I was able and willing to do the 'care-taking' job in the summer as well. This was unusual, for normally it was only in Winter that she went away. However, knowing that I was to be working close by on the mainland in Naplos in mid-September, and mindful of the cost of keeping my house in Yorkshire, I was grateful for the chance to stay in a convenient part of Greece which I liked, and to let my tenants have another term in my bungalow. I began to get used to the idea of staying in Greece for the Summer.

A bit of fencing work which had to be done in the top field

where the olive trees were had been waiting for Elsie's return. She duly called upon the services of one Spiros, who turned out to be one of the legions of willing but put-upon Albanian workers under-pinning the practical end of Greek life. These workers had come from a country whose draconian regime left the economic migrants in fear for their families back home, while feeling bound to work abroad away from them to gain enough money to keep them from poverty.

That the situation has changed for the better now both within Albania and in terms of the rights and proper wages of the Albanian workers in Greece is a good thing in humanitarian terms, but a worry for the Greek government. For here, to name two examples, we have the problem of the British with the large Asian communities, and of the Germans with the Turkish immigrants. In Greece, not only is there the resentment against people taking jobs in difficult times, but also a very real perception that with the Albanian immigration came a great increase in the crime rate, certainly in Athens. Unfortunately for their honest hard-working countrymen, the criminal element who were released along with the political prisoners have ruined the reputation of all.

But in those days, I was fascinated with this man who had left his family to come and work all hours abroad, seemingly learning Greek in a beat in order to do so. Given my struggles with the language I was particularly in awe of this. However, I have since learnt that many of these 'Albanians' are from what was once part of Greece, trapped in another country by the propensity of the Great Powers to change the boundaries in the Balkan countries for whatever the current expediency is. So they were likely to have some knowledge of Greek already, and have been brought up as Orthodox Christians, and thus even more attracted to trying their luck in Greece. (The Albanians in general are predominantly Muslim.) I know of one man one man (a 'true' Albanian, and Muslim) who kept walking over the mountains barefoot when his shoes disintegrated, so determined was he to be free.

Elsie and Spiros managed to communicate in a very simple Greek, Elsie's Oxbridge accent unmitigated in the foreign tongue, to curious effect. The work was duly done, in quick time, and for little money. So we have the usual pattern, that the immigrants do the menial jobs which the rest of the population don't want to do for reasons of snobbishness, laziness or whatever. Certainly, and I am sorry to have to say it, the Albanian workers are willing to work regularly, for long hours, unlike the Greeks who tend to be lazy, and unconcerned about getting things done on time. This, of course, rebounds on them when it DOES matter. Who can forget the panic in Athens over the Olympic Games? That it all came out all right in the end involved hidden sacrifices by others.

Is it generally known that the citizens of Gotenborg in Sweden had to do without their new trams because it had not occurred to the Greeks that an order had to be placed earlier than 3 months in advance? German construction workers were the heroes of the finished stadia and Metro. It really makes you want to shake the collective Greek nation, for they will walk away from it all with a charming smile and a shrug - it was ok, was it not? - or, worse, boast about how great it all was. Well yes, because everyone else helped you out.

So Spiros came to help Elsie out. And I continued to do so, though living with her brought the occasional clash.

Though living mainly at opposite ends of the I-shaped house, we did have to share the main kitchen, where my occasional neglect of the washing up would lead to lectures about ants. (Of course I thought this was a bit rich coming from the woman whose filthy outside kitchen I had scrubbed). We did have fun with the hairdresser when she came to 'do' us both, and gave me a shorter style which I could 'scrunch' into waviness.

Elsie could behave very oddly sometimes, as in when I took her into town one afternoon. When things did not go perfectly as she had planned they would, in terms of where we were to park, she tried to insist on being taken home. This was a ludicrous waste of time for both of us, and I refused. I told her she should just get on and do what she had come down for. At least she had the good grace to admit later that I had been right to be firm with her. Elsie was clearly a control freak, but I had managed to survive the first skirmish. What would come next?

It was not long before matters came to a head. While I had been out at work, Elsie had had to go into my bedroom, to look for a book which she thought was on one of the over-bed shelves. Now I am a soul who likes to be well turned out, but I am capable of leaving my bedroom in an untidy state. I returned in the evening fairly late, after being out with Sofia, and did not see Elsie till the next morning, when I greeted her as normal, expecting to be engaged on some useful, possibly mutual, task. Imagine my shock when she suddenly faced me with having changed her mind about my doing the job at her estate in the Summer, and, incredibly to me, gave her reason as

'I couldn't bear the mess.'

After all I had done, this required a thousand-word answer or none. I was stung, betrayed, very hurt. All I could get out was,

'Right, I am going then.'

I then proceeded to hurl my possessions, unpacked, as quickly as possible, into the car, all the time seething on the verge of tears. My task was somewhat impeded by a regretful Elsie who trotted about after me interjecting,

'Oh, please don't go!' amid my snarls of

'I have to. What did you expect?'

Finally, having decided I had probably got everything important, I roared off up the dirt track. I would need to return the car of course, and that would be a time to reclaim any overlooked belongings. I was quite glad that when I did come back a few days later at the weekend Elsie had her neighbour round for coffee. With Elsie occupied, I was able to have a look round in peace and get, for example, my set of plates, which I had not been able to pack before. A quick goodbye, and off down the track to get the bus from the junction.

It was at the WI the following Friday that I had the conversation with Andrew which (given those meaningful looks back in January) he had known was coming all along. It turned out he had once done the job for Elsie, so he knew how she would react to my efforts.

'The only way I stayed friends with her was to leave the instant she got back. We were all amazed and full of admiration that you managed to stay on. And it lasted - what - 10 days?'

So of course we had the conversation about how Elsie said she was keen on people making improvements, but at the same time was super-threatened by everyone being able to run the place better than she herself. So she got one's services, but could not help picking a fight to get rid of one. Little wonder she did not have a regular helper. They had all been burnt already.

The next time that I heard from her, she admitted that she was impossible to live with. And, under her regime, the hens were once more getting out and pooping all over the place. So much for my scratches and tussles with the wire. But funnily enough she had decided to get good old Spiros to make the hens' enclosure smaller, as per my son James's suggestion. Over the years, I have not had much news from her, though it seems she sold some of the land to make building repairs and buy a better vehicle. Well, despite a reasonable expectation that Elsie's alcohol consumption would finish her, it seems its preservative qualities have come to the fore. Indeed, only a few months ago, I chanced to meet a young man from the island whose parents lived near Elsie and who said she was still going strong. Maybe I will write again.

Though traumatised initially by my break-up with Elsie, I must say it was convenient to be in the flat again, and handy for any tasks Sofia might call me to. I had been working mainly with the Michigan class, for their high level exams, including orals, were approaching and the more practice they had in conversation the better. I had also tried to help my Greek teacher Thassoula with her Cambridge English, but this, like my Greek lessons, was a sporadic affair. The Cambridge exam is not for the faint-hearted, and indeed I would say that about half of English A level students would struggle with it.

During these few days in early May, I had dinner with

Sally, the sporty girl and travel representative I had met through the tennis club. We were in the fish taverna on the sloping cobbled path above the harbour side. I was facing up the slope, towards the marble display on which many fish were laid. My concentration on Sally wavered when, over her shoulder, I caught sight of first one, then the other, of the large lobsters in the centre, slowly beginning to crawl away down the slab. The first one had reached the edge and dropped to the cobbles, and the other was teetering on the edge, by the time the head waiter spotted them and replaced them on their perch to await their doom. Dear me, how upsetting that they were still alive, though very weakened. How could this be? Presumably enough water is trapped in their shells for them to absorb some oxygen to keep them going for a while. It really was a bit of a shock, for it must be cruel to keep them in what, for us, would be in a state of near drowning. At least they could have kept them in a tank, like fish which are about to be selected by a diner. It nearly turned me vegetarian. But I fear it says something about the Greek attitude to animal life in general, which is not to recognise feelings, but to regard them kind of living machines for the use of human beings.

This incident occupied our conversation for some time, but eventually Sally got onto what was her business for the evening. I had, naturally, told her what had happened with Elsie and that I was now left with no house to go back to in the UK and nothing to do until the middle of September. Sally took a breath,

'How do you fancy being the rep on Kalkos?'

'Where's that?'

'It's a little island in the Dodecanese. I've just been

there for a while and it's gorgeous.'

'Well I've often noticed the girls being reps in the summer and wondered about doing it.'

'I think you would be good.'

'Thanks! But I can only do it till mid - September. Will that be any good?'

'I'll ask my boss. I'm sure they could sort something out.'

'Ok, thanks. You can tell them I'm interested.'

So Sally went off and spoke to Head Office, who asked for a fax of my CV. They then duly phoned me up at the *frontistirio*, to interview me. They assured me that they could cover late September till October, and when could I start? Good question, which depended on Sofia. That good lady, ever helpful, and probably glad to have off her hands one who was increasingly a 'spare part' agreed to release me early. Once that was settled, Sally and I had another meeting for her to brief me about the island, the set up she had found there in the agency, the initial work she had done, and what my duties would be. Sitting in the bar, a little nervous, absorbing information, I hardly realised what had begun for me.

CHAPTER 12 - COMING TO KALKOS

Sarah made it quite clear that she thought I was very lucky to be going to this fabulous place. Indeed, she wanted to stay there herself. But it would have made no sense for someone experienced in Stargos and its sister islands to move to a new one, while an inexperienced rep took over from her. Clearly the place exerted a pull on people. I was intrigued. Yes, it looked pretty in the photos from the company's brochure, but there had to be more to it.

I was nervous at the idea of making my mark in a new job area (though used to working with people). I had to take a group to the airport and send them safely home, and meet others to take them across to the island and into their villas - on only my third day in the job. I was assured that the agency people knew all about me and were waiting eagerly for me to take up the responsibility, which the company had previously hoped to devolve on the agents themselves. This had led to a warning that the loyalty of the clients would be lost to other companies, who were able to offer a personal service.

Judging by the way Sarah had been doing things, unburdened by standardised forms, I could see that one had a lot of freedom and scope for creativity. Indeed she encouraged me to develop my own style and improve on the quick setting-up job she had had to do before her own season started. She told me that the company was small but genuine, and well worth my best efforts and support.

As for my likely clients, they seemed to be of a certain character, mainly middle class professionals - and all British. Indeed the strangest thing about the island was that almost all the tourists were British and nearly all of that certain grouping, veering to the 50 plus age group. Clearly this was a different kind of rep's job, and all to the good. Someone with culture and maturity was needed to work with clients like this. Not wishing to be unkind, the image of the usual 'rep' is of a 20 year old lad or lass with a chirpy manner and a mission to sell tours (and sometimes, on the darker side, a plan to get the boys and girls drunk and put them together.)

After a couple of days packing up my stuff and cleaning the flat, all the while reflecting on the new demands to be place on me, I was ready both physically and mentally for Sarah to take me to the airport. It was a Monday, the 23rd of May, a date forever etched in the memory. This was my first (and thankfully last) experience of Stargos Airport, with its wickedly short runway and its notoriously small departure halls, not to mention the eccentric screens which announced planes going to Thessaloniki via Oslo. (Thessaloniki being the refuelling spot for the international planes forced to take off from Stargos with a low fuel load to manage it at all.)

An amazing scene met me round in the valley. People were spread all over the grass banks, with their luggage, or ensconced in the cluster of tavernas and cafes which had grown up on the valley slope across from a terminal building which was ridiculously small for the job it had to do. Well I suppose, with so little flat land available for runway, they could hardly use more of it for a bigger building. It turned out that, once one had checked in, there was so little room over at the gate side that they could not let people through passport control until just before the plane was due to board. This made the whole business rather tense for the reps I am sure, for one did not want one's group to disperse and lose track of time. So the responsibility for finding them all and making sure they turned up for gate time, would be an extra burden most travel representatives were not used to, for normally one can say goodbye once boarding cards have been achieved.

Sarah, of course, was a veteran of the place and soon guided me through what I needed to do there and in Athens, where I would transfer. At least my considerable baggage was checked all the way through. Once again assured about my boat, and that I was being looked out for, and with promises to keep in touch exchanged, I kissed Sarah goodbye and thanks and went through to board my small plane. Athens airport seemed a blur, and soon I was landing again at Rhodes, with a feeling of tension about missing the boat. Good grief, it was already 2 o' clock and my luggage had not all emerged - and the boat went at 2.30 from a port a 30 minute taxi ride away. Well somehow I struggled out with all my stuff and into a taxi. I must have been lucky, for usually they did not like going South to the little port, with little chance of a return fare.

The minutes were ticking away, however, and there seemed no hope, good driver though he was, of us making the boat in time. I had not learned the ways of Kalkos and its people yet, of course - or the virtues of what a good friend of mine calls GMT - 'Greek Maybe Time'. We roared down the admittedly lovely coastline. Leaving behind larger settlements with tourist apartments we found smaller and smaller villages, sandy cliffs with goats, isolated beach tavernas, and splendid tree and vine clad mountains with market gardens and bush vineyards on the lower slopes and the flat strip of land beside the sea. But so tense was I that I barely registered all this changing beauty and how it spoke of the richness and variety of what was to become my 'mainland'.

At last, we turned for the port, and to my amazement and great joy, the boat was still there. Well, naturally, this was because Kostas, the agent's father who had been sent to look out for me, had asked them to wait. It was important I did not lose a day of preparation given the need for me to spring into action as a competent 'rep' by the Wednesday. So it seemed, with boats at least, things could be made flexible when required. I was surprised and a little embarrassed when applause broke out as I exited the taxi. Here I was starring in a little Greek drama, with Kostas beaming me aboard as my leading man (for now).

The journey of an hour and a quarter passed with beer refreshment and good conversation, for Kosta's English was excellent, he having worked with the radio service 'Voice of America' for years. He answered many questions, explained many things I needed to know about the operation of the agency, and the set-up on the island, and pointed out sights on Rhodes and the other islands we passed. The sea was gloriously calm, the light fabulous, but I was beginning to notice a difference in the landscape of the islands. Stargos had been heavily wooded, very green. Rhodes was less wooded, but still a green island. But the smaller islands here were bare and rocky, with few trees and only light scrubby vegetation. Was this a feature of the hotter drier climate down in these islands, or was it a legacy, as with many, of the Greek's plundering of their own trees to make ships? They little realised the ecological effects, when lack of trees caused soil erosion, and trees became no longer viable on the land.

At first, on the journey, I was aware of other islands in the distance, but the first we passed turned out to be a deserted island, a place of great historical interest, which I was assured I would get to visit. In the distance, half an hour's sailing beyond, rose up another island, of quite imposing shape: Kalkos. A small sharp peak was flanked across the valley by a taller, rounded mountain. Goodness, it seemed very high. The photos in the company brochure had given no clue of how mountainous it was for its tiny size (20km long at its maximum by 4 km wide). Coming nearer, one could see how the mountain formed a backdrop to the village which was arranged in an amphitheatre around a semicircular bay.

The sharp peak resolved itself into a crag with the remains of castle wall on top, shaped almost like a gently crooked finger, and with a window opening showing blue sky behind. To the right, the trees clustered in the valley made welcome contrast of green against the great beige, golden and grey expanses of rock elsewhere. To the left, the skyline was interrupted by 3 stone windmills on the ridge, red-roofed but with no sails.

Below, the amphitheatre shape of the village started to become clearer. In mellow stone and white and many colours, the houses were piled behind each other, many ruins among them, up the slopes around the harbour. The effect was at once elegant and quaint and stunningly pretty. Here was a place to make the eyes greedy. They could not get enough of its colours, textures, shapes, constantly changing with the light. But there was something else to account for that shiver down my spine. Was it grandeur? Awe? The alien aspect of the mountain, bare, inhospitable, set against the loveliness of the little village, such a tribute to human artistry, emphasised the puniness of human beings in such an environment. This would be living on an edge, carving out an existence in a landscape tolerating its inhabitants, setting them constant challenges.

Individual buildings started to become clearer. A large structure, several buildings joined, occupying the left hand end of the bay, turned out to be the Hotel, composed, in the centre part, of one of the old sponge-fishing warehouses. In the centre of the village, I could see a stone clock tower and, nearby, a white building reminiscent of a wedding cake, which proved to be the Town Hall. It had a pair of rather splendid Venetian looking snake - curving steps leading up to its high position. But even more striking was the Church, almost at the waterside at the right of the harbour-front. Elegant in white and yellow and blue, the tall bell tower, stone-based, was attached to a large main building with a double curved dark red roof. The whole was set off by the tall, dark green candle flame shape of the magnificent courtyard conifer. There were trees attractively

interspersed among the restaurants and bars of the harbour-front, and clustered in the small town square which lay behind the great concrete tongue of the jetty, for one side of which our boat was headed, to her regular mooring.

As many before and since, I was entranced by the beauty and glorious setting of this village. The sparkling cerulean water, the bright jumble of fishing boats, the mellow stone and colourful paint invited many closer looks. And always one could lift one's gaze to the mountain, watching over us, impassively waiting. But I had neither the time nor the energy to explore immediately. First stop was the agency office, at the back of the main square, next to a small supermarket, and adjoining the most traditional-looking of the tavernas, set under the trees.

Here I was introduced to Helen (who had anglicised her name from Eleni) who ran the agency representing the company I was to work for. Also in the agency was a much larger company which had been in the business of villa holidays on the island for about 7 years. And here were my closest colleagues, and yet competitors, two women with whom I was destined to work, cooperate, travel, socialise. Jill and Maggie, both attractive blondes of 'a certain age' were friendly and welcoming, though I was surprised to find that Maggie, the more outgoing of the two, was not the boss. Jill was naturally shyer, and, Maggie had to warn me, suffering a great deal owing to the tragic death of her husband only two months previously.

I found the details of my clients, whom I would take to the airport two days later. They were a group of painters, led by a male tutor whom I will call Mr W. I prepared their transfer, contacting our agents in Rhodes to order taxis, and putting them on the luggage transfer list. To my great delight, they were having an exhibition that very evening at one of the bars, so I hurried along there to make their acquaintance and give them details of their departure arrangements, a rather depressing thing to do 2 days before, I thought, but in fact people like to know what is happening, for then they can relax.

I was somewhat surprised by the tutor's appearance, being as he wore a red patterned handkerchief as a rather piratical-looking headband. Well, it takes all sorts. The pictures were lovely, especially his, in soft pastel, which inspired me to do some work in that medium myself. When Wednesday came, the reason for the headband become clear, for, when he took it off, I found that he had been concealing a rather alarming large scab on his head. It turned out that he had taken the group up to the *Kastro* on the preceding Saturday, and had misjudged a doorway into the chapel, banging his head severely. So I was quite lucky that, firstly, he had done this before I got there and had to cope with it, and secondly, that he had not been seriously injured.

All went smoothly with the transfer, by taxis from the little harbour to the airport, where I was to help at the check in, then go and meet the incoming flight. I did not have many villas to look after, only 9 separate accommodations, some within the same building. And only 1, which I had managed to visit and check out, was to be occupied in the coming week. So it was a couple whom I met off the flight and duly accompanied to the port, to await the departure of the boat. This could be a bit tedious, especially if the flight was early, as the charter boat was timed to wait for much later flights. Still it was not a bad place to wait, and the most sensible clients decided to regard it as the start of their holiday, a nice lunch at a little harbour. Views of glistening blue water and the rugged coastline of Rhodes formed a backdrop to the occupations of the local fishermen, mending or sorting nets, tinkering with boats and so on.

I talked a bit to the clients on the way over, but, always mindful that they were a bit sleepy, having got up very early for the flight, arranged to see them the next day once they had had a rest, and could thus take in the information better. I could then gather my thoughts for the rest of the voyage, preparing for the show-in to their accommodation. It was still a novelty to me then, the trip over, and the exhilarating beauty of the place. I kept reliving it through the eyes of my clients. We deposited the luggage on the quayside for delivery by the little 3 wheeled truck, and set off walking up through the narrow streets and stone steps to the house. Once there, I explained the basics of how to work the hot water and the shutters, a reminder not to flush the toilet paper (what a country) and so on. The clients had a 'welcome pack' with water, wine, tea and coffee, bread cheese etc, so they could have a simple supper 'at home' if wished, but most went out quickly to try one of the tavernas before an early night and a refreshed morrow.

Once I had made my villa visits, I would not have much to do, unless there was a crisis, for our whole approach, across all the companies, was very much 'hands off'. The other companies had welcome meetings, but, small as we were, it was left to the representatives to find their own style, and I was happier, as were the clients, with individual meetings at the house, when I could tailor my information to their needs. There was no pushy salesmanship, no cheesy community activities. Kalkos was a class act. We did have one excursion, a picnic on the neighbouring deserted island, which I had to publicise and hope to sell (if only to get the numbers up to make it viable) and that was it. Occasionally, one of the boats would do a round the island trip or such, but this was generally a turn up if you wish casual affair, not requiring forward planning and food ordering like the picnic.

So, Thursday morning visits and Sunday picnics aside, my time was spent in the office going over the information which Sarah had prepared, and trying to improve it. Here was the first difficulty with working in the same office as the other company. Naturally, Sarah had had to get her information from somewhere, and it seemed she had had a lot of help from what was of course a rival company. It was not made clear to me at the time, but Jill in particular had built up a bit of resentment about what she saw as plagiarism of the information she had gathered and written. I think on reflection that Sarah should have openly acknowledged in our files to clients that we were indebted to the other company.

One great mistake I did make, however, was to be too eager to engage clients who were not mine. It was more excusable if they spoke to me, assuming me to be another worker for that company. But I cringe now to think of the times when (because I was under-employed, bored, keen, whatever), I would join in exchanges between Jill or Maggie, or both, and their clients. Now it seems that they were complaining about me behind my back to the agent, but she did not directly speak to me about the matter for quite a while. I would rather have known from the beginning, for the atmosphere would have been better.

CHAPTER 13 - MEETING THE COMMUNITY

Socially, everything was fine, largely due to Maggie, with whom I instinctively got on. She had had an extraordinary life, beginning as a stable girl who married the boss's son (but later divorced after having one son). Her second marriage, to a farmer, also foundered, at which point she took off for a life at sea, gaining her master's papers, and crewing around the Mediterranean, based for many years in Malta. Amazingly, though she learnt the difficult language Maltese she could not get to grips with Greek at all. Maggie had been living in Lindos on Rhodes, caretaking houses and crewing boats, when she was recruited by the boss of the company who had a house there, to be Jill's work partner. I was somewhat in awe of Maggie's confidence and also her facility with men, which made me a bit puzzled (given that she was about 8 years older than me) and envious. I had a lot to learn.

I did not learn much about Jill, who kept herself to herself apart from certain of her inner circle. It seemed she had been a librarian in the UK, and had met and fallen for her eventual husband, a fisherman, while she was on holiday on Kalkos with some female friends. That they had had only a few years together by the time they managed to marry was a great tragedy, but cancer is no respecter of anyone's merit in life. Jill had acquired a new extended Greek family, and a great facility in Greek, over the years, and then, on Yianni's passing, inherited his little house. Her life was on Kalkos, and her employment, and so she was determined to stay.

Pretty well as soon as I arrived, I was introduced to Phil and Sally, the couple who represented the largest company running villa holidays on the island. They were based in another agency. But nothing is very far from anywhere else on Kalkos. They were lively, friendly, welcoming. Phil was energetic, funny, with striking blue eyes (which could become ice if he was angry with you) and lovely curly grey hair which (probably because of his Navy background), he would insist on having cut very short, just when it was getting to a flattering and more sensual length. He had retired from the Navy and gone into a surplus supplies business, but soon the call to wander as he had all his life was too strong, and his marriage having ended in divorce, he went after and got the Kalkos job.

But he needed a partner, and a female one at that, for the company liked to have couples as their representatives. Certainly, a man/woman team has advantages in dealing with any problems that arise. That the representatives were usually a married couple was another thing. It could be a strain on the marriage, and people did not usually last long in what was quite a demanding and stressful job. Phil was lucky in that he had met Sally in his home town in the West Country, and, having helped her through a crisis, felt able to call on her support. Although already working as the representative for another company, Sally resigned from that, and came to join

Phil on Kalkos. If Maggie had had an eventful life, Sally's was mind-boggling. Born in Scotland daughter of an airforce-man, she had been sent to boarding school at only 7 years old, and had a lasting resentment of her less than motherly mother. Sally had travelled all over the world independently, worked in the hotel trade in Australia and finally set up a hotel in her West Country home town. Tragically, the hotel burned down, and, even worse, was uninsured (a swindle by her business partner). So a traumatised Sally found herself taking work as a 'trolley dolly' on the trains, serving drinks and snacks. No wonder she needed Phil's help and moral support.

The couple lived together, for they were 'an item', in a little villa just above the harbour-front, which became a favourite haunt of all of us for get-togethers. The pair had only arrived in the March so, like me, they were new to their job. But they had about 45 accommodations to take care of, not 9 like me, so they were very busy. And in those days they used to do villa visits to everyone at least once a week, so a day off was an unknown concept. But their hard work paid off in their popularity with their clients. Sally with her educated accent, her pretty face (and voluptuous figure), lively personality, was the organiser, efficient, charming, great in a crisis, while Phil was 'Mr Personality' the showy one with the hearty jocular approach. Both were intelligent and funny, and if I tended to gravitate to their company it was probably because I saw so much of Jill and Maggie during office hours. All in all, we all got on well as a happy gang in much the same boat.

One person I became aware of but did not see much of was Cathy, who worked in the office for Phil and Sally when they were out on villa visits, excursions, or transfers. She was a very well-spoken, quiet girl, a petite blonde well-matched to her very attractive (if small) and charming Greek partner Nikitas. They kept themselves to themselves socially, but it soon became known to me that Nikitas was a vitally important person to know and cultivate on the island. He was our local 'Mr Fix-it' and unlike the normal members of 'bodgers united' he knew what he was doing. He would also turn out for emergency duty out of hours if electrical or plumbing disasters occurred.

My little house, for which I had to top up the rent, was rather cute, if a bit hot, all its windows facing South. It was a villa useless for tourists, having no view, but very handy for the harbour and the office, though a bit too handy for the path going past to the end of the village and the Hotel beyond. It was not a great house for entertaining, being rather small and having nowhere to sit outside. Indeed, when I wanted to make efforts to exercise to maintain fitness and stave off some of the effects of the social eating and drinking, I was forced to do it in the street in full view of the somewhat bemused locals. The thought of actually walking in the heat appals most Greeks, never mind the idea of jogging on the spot, skipping etc.

I did try to have one dinner party. But it was just too hot for everybody, though they tried politely. And I had not realised that Jill could not eat my speciality, Chinese-American marinated spare rib chops, as she never ate pork. Thank goodness I had made chick pea and apricot casserole and red cabbage with apple, 2 other favourites, as well as mixed salad, so there were plenty of other choices.

A rather startling factor was that when the big boat came in, the inter-island ferry, the whole house would be shaking. This was extremely worrying to one who knew that Greece could be an earthquake zone, but had never experienced one. The first time, I simply had to dash out to see what was happening, for I could not see out of the high window up at the ceiling which faced the harbour. Good grief! There appeared to be an enormous multi-storey building attempting to enter the harbour. It towered over the first 3 ranks of houses, and its huge engines were obviously responsible for churning up the water to such an extent that the artificially-extended paved harbour-front was no protection from the vibration. Even now, many years later, the magic of seeing the giant ship manoeuvring to visit little Kalkos has never palled. Because I was likely to have little privacy if I opened the shutters and windows, I devised various methods of overcoming this, to allow myself air without being on public view. Several of my sarongs ended up doing duty as 'net curtains', while, when it was windy, I found that tying the main curtains together stopped them from blowing in or out of the window, causing a sudden exposure of my possibly unclad or bed-ensconced self.

I had picked the house partly because it had a good oven, not necessarily for the meal preparation potential, but because one of the art activities I was starting was the painting of ceramics, which could be home fired for durability. Unfortunately, along with the good oven came an exceptionally noisy old fridge, large but obviously with rather hardened arteries. I used to put it on during the times when I was going to be out, or was going to be playing music, but at other times such as the 'siesta' break 2.30 to 5 in the afternoon, and during the night, I could not stand to listen to its incisive buzzing and vibrating. Maggie used to joke with me that she could hear it from a long way off when walking through the village, and would remark to herself, 'Ah, Fran's got the fridge on again.'

One of the features of the house which I had not met before was that the bathroom had no shower stall, just a drain in the floor - yes, a wet room, invented by the Greeks well ahead of the fashion. This took a bit of getting used to, as did the sudden interruptions in the water supply. Luckily, on the day when the water went off mid shower when I was covered in foam, I had been a responsible citizen shortly before, and saved the rinsing water from my washing to use for plant watering, loo flushing etc. So I used it for rinsing me instead.

This water conservation was an approach we recommended to all our clients, who responded cooperatively. They realised that, on an island where every drop of water in the mains had to be brought in by tanker, economy was paramount. The only trouble was, everywhere on the island one could witness maids and householders splashing water about with reckless abandon; embarrassing in view of our message. The preferred method of patio cleaning is to chase down the dust with a hose rather than sweeping and later mopping as would be responsible. It was especially infuriating if hoses were left running while the person did something else, or, worse, left the premises. My blood pressure would suffer as I fulminated to myself and others (if possible, to the person involved) that this was why the island ran out of water, and so on. I'm afraid it is a classic case of the sort of mentality all too common in Greece which goes something like this. Look after yourself. Do not feel responsible for the wellbeing of anyone else. Do not consider other people's needs. As long as you are all right yourself and have what you need to be comfortable, everything is ok.

I was embraced into the social scene, and soon met others, like Jenny, an English girl who worked at one of the bars, and Karen, the first Englishwoman to settle on the island, running a boarding house since the early 80s with her Greek ex-Navy husband. Jenny had come to Kalkos some 12 years before, when only 19. Originally from the Birmingham area, she had lived in Ionannina in Northern Greece where she worked, in a jewellery shop and as a furniture restorer. But the magic of Kalkos had won her heart and her loyalty, as had her partner Giorgos, who worked as head waiter in one of the tavernas. She also found a surrogate mother in Karen. Jenny's own mother had died very young, and the experience of this serious illness and of nursing a loved one when still only a child herself had had a profound effect, and sent her to find a new life abroad. She was still very friendly with her father, who would often come to visit.

Karen had come on holiday to Rhodes in about 1980, in the days when there was little tourist activity on Kalkos. She had come over for a few days to the boarding house run by Tomas, recently retired from the Navy and recently bereaved, his wife having been killed in a plane crash. Karen's marriage was breaking up. She and Tomas began a friendship which soon developed, and two years later they were married and Karen moved to Kalkos to help him run the boarding house. In the Winter, they moved to his flat in Athens. Tomas was 'an international Greek' as I call it, a highly educated man, retired at the rank of rear-Admiral. He spoke several languages fluently, notably English and Italian, but also French and German. He spoke of how he loved to be able to talk to his guests in their own languages, and how much they appreciated this. Tomas was real 'Kalkos royalty' with a pedigree including the war hero featured on the World War II memorial, the first Greek officer killed in the conflict. As such, he was always the one to lay the wreath on behalf of the people of Kalkos on remembrance days. Tomas and Karen's boarding house was another great social setting for all of us 'ex-pats' though Tomas could sometimes get fed up with the English-speaking company which gathered round his charming and friendly wife.

Down on the harbour-front, there was a little shop, a dangerous place to visit as it was full of desirable things, such as earrings and candles. I used to joke with Joan, the owner, that I did not like coming to see her as it turned out too expensive. Joan was a striking woman in her early 60s who had been a personal assistant in the Foreign Service, in the Middle East for many years, and had later gone to live on a larger island nearby for a few years, before finding Kalkos, and opening a small gift shop. I responded to the good taste of the items she stocked. My first aim was to get her to sell some of my paintings, but she was not keen to deal in artwork. An idea began to form in my mind.

An early challenge (and here my book on Greek Men should have helped me) was to deal with the amorous advances of some of the local males. I had been warned by Sarah about one guy in particular. Obviously, when she was visiting from Stargos, Nikos the fisherman had targeted her pretty quickly. Well he was onto me within a few days. One night, he had accosted me at the table when I was finishing my dinner. I am naturally friendly, so I was not going to be rude. But sadly, even passing the time of day can be taken as encouragement by these guys. I was making my way back to my villa, when all of a sudden I was accosted on the path in the dark by the fisherman. It is a good job the wine had relaxed me, for I startle easily. For the life of me I can't remember what I said, but I managed to get rid of him. I did not feel threatened in terms of being attacked, but just annoyed that I had to deal with a nuisance.

One was beginning to understand why the large company favoured married couples or at least secure partnerships for its representatives. Romantic, or at least physical, entanglements with the local males were clearly a hazard for single women. Single men, however, would face a dual problem. They might well be attractive to the local girls, but the girls' families would not favour such associations. As for relationships with clients, it was made crystal clear to me that this was a sacking offence, at least from my company's standpoint.

There were 3 British men who made it to my doorstep (but not beyond), none of them my own clients. Phil (who never let a handy woman go to waste) gave me a goodnight kiss after he walked me home from a very late session in a bar, and indeed the same thing happened with David, the teacher, who took a fancy to me. But the third guy was a strange example. We had been to Alimnia on the picnic and this visitor (abandoning his wife) insisted on carrying my bag back to my door, despite my protests that I only lived a step away and could manage perfectly well thank you. I need not have been alarmed, however, by his intentions, as his aim was to engage me in a long and boring doorstep conversation - about drains. Evidently, being confronted with Kalkos's strange plumbing and drains had awakened the obsessive professional in this drain specialist. He harangued me for some time about how he would be glad to give his services, and those of his robot remote drain-investigating device, to assist the community in sorting out its pipe-work problems. Finally, my eyes glazing over and swaying with fatigue, I managed to halt the flow and bid him goodbye. It became evident that, for the period of the holiday, his wife had banned him from talking about drains, and I was a friendly 'mother confessor' when the pressure of his obsession grew too much.

As for obsession, I fell under the spell of Nektarios, one of the taverna owners, a tall handsome (if slightly chubby) guy with the killer equipment of big brown eyes and dazzling smile. As my Greek was so pitiful at this time, we communicated mostly in French as he seemed to prefer this to English, having worked in French-speaking areas of North Africa. The whole relationship was fairly unsatisfactory, especially as taverna work does not lend itself to any sort of social life - at least not at normal waking hours. There was also plenty of what I would call 'blowing hot and cold'. I never knew where I was with him, which led to a lot of heartache. Maggie had had a fling with him herself, and was helpful in making me realise that he was the strange one in the relationship, not me.

I was getting to know some of the other male figures around the village, thankfully not in a romantic context. One of the most striking was Alexandros the Mayor, with a nose as big as his personality and his reputation as a womaniser. He was also the agent for the tour company Phil and Sally worked for. Then there was Andreas the fisherman, long retired, silver-haired, permanently in a cap. He had a ready smile and a cheeky sparkle, a facility in English and an eye for the ladies - especially generously-built blondes. I was in some danger here. Giorgos the shop-keeper was also very attentive to older ladies, and one had to put up with a bit of fairly mild groping till one got the message across that one was not interested, at which point he reverted to merely verbal stroking.

Much younger, and a bit shy, was Tasos, the island's postman, who dispensed the mail (which everyone collected themselves), dealt with bills and the post office bank. Tasos was very attractive, but a little sad, for he was lonely, having found no girlfriend on Kalkos. Another striking figure was the priest, also young, and, it turned out, an *archimandritis* which meant he was at a high level of training, too senior really to be a village priest, but on the island because of his family connections, and because he loved it so. He was a great charmer, and never short of female company, although he had obviously taken the decision long ago that he would never marry. Married men can become priests, but they can never progress up the ranks, nor can an existing priest decide to get married. The Pappas had done much in his short time (he was in his third year on Kalkos) to make the church much more popular. Attendance at services had soared, and charitable works had taken off. It was a golden period, to have such a clever young man, so committed to the island, pouring his energy into the job.

In the agency, Kostas, Helen's father, was on duty quite a lot of the time, and often grumpy about it, for he was supposed to be retired. He could be impatient and short-tempered, and disinclined to put himself out too much to sort out problems. It was all a feature of his daughter's putting a load on him because she could not be there, having a young child, and a sea captain husband based in Rhodes. Sadly, there seemed to be something about me that irritated him, and he would pick me up on things I had said, and criticise the way I went about the job. For example my struggles with the ancient clanking old fax machine he had landed me with were met with scorn and derision. So it seems he was not the Kostas for this particular Shirley Valentine.

Luckily Kosta's wife Maria was as calm, patient and charming as he was not, so when she was around she smoothed his moods and greatly improved the atmosphere in the office. They had four children, with Helen the only girl. So there were quite a few in the extended family to get to know. The eldest son was married, and a policeman. Helen was married to Yiannis, the son of Giorgos the shopkeeper. Marcos the third child was working in Rhodes, while Vangelis the youngest was still at school. Helen had studied Hotel Management in Florida, so was expert in English, as was her mother, who was one of the top guides in Rhodes, fluent in about 5 languages. I found that many older Greeks had particular skills in Italian, and soon discovered that this was because of the background of the islands, having been under Italian rule for many years, and the Greek children having been forced to attend school in Italian. Needless to say, as often happens, it was the Church (in an underground way) that ensured that the children kept in touch with their own native language.

So I was being embraced by various 'families', the people in the agency and their connections, the ex-pats, and the Greeks I dealt with every day. But there was one large group I was to see a lot of, in the bars and tavernas of the island.

CHAPTER 14 - EATING AND DRINKING

The centre of Kalkos night life in those days was the bar nearest the Church, where Michalis and his partner Manolis, a big jolly character, presided over a large area of comfortable cane chairs, usually populated with large groups of British tourists. This was the place for late night conversation usually over a few Metaxas (fine at the time, lethal in the morning). I sat one night with Phil (Sally having retired earlier) until 3.00 a.m. and then managed to leave my shirt behind (worn over a dress - I was decent) and kept forgetting to pick it up. Despite being deprived of his sleep, Manolis loyally held onto the shirt for me till I remembered about it. Here one could have a great game of pool, an ice cream, a cake.

Further along the harbour-front was a lovely bar with a stone central counter, and attractive vine-type plants above, serving the best draught beer in town, even if the old director's chairs were not notable for comfort. This was the realm of Andonis and his family. Andonis had been one of the heart-throbs of the island in his younger days, and had kept his figure and a certain swarthy sexiness. His wife (a bit of a dragon), kept a close watch on things, while son Valandis and daughter Christina helped their father.

It was a parents and son team who ran the next bar, a favourite haunt of the early morning travellers, and the late night card players, a long day for the bar. Just as well they had Yiannis the son, Athina the mother and Christos the father to share the load. It was here, for one of the last times it happened on Kalkos (village habits giving way to changing mores due to tourism) that I witnessed a dance in 'the ring of fire' when some of the company pour spirit on the floor in a circle. A dancer enters the circle and it is lit, whereupon he performs inside the fire. This applies only to male solo dancing (a novel concept to those of us from the UK where the function of a male at a dance is usually to prop up the bar while watching the females dance round their handbags.)

Sadly, even then, the spontaneity of Greek night life had abandoned Kalkos. Gone were the days when the local musicians would congregate in a *kafenion* and an impromptu session start, with the local people coming along and dancing. This was a time before street lighting, only introduced (fairly minimally) in the late 80s. Television and computers were unknown, both of which have been the death of so much social interaction in other countries. There had, however, once been a cinema, in the long building, later divided and rented as studios, near the Church. It used to slightly embarrass the travel representatives that we had to explain to visitors that they were unlikely to experience 'live' local music and dancing unless it was an organised event. And, worse, we discovered that the musicians expected to be paid. I always used to get on my high horse and opine that they should play for free for the joy of it and the good of the village, a view stronger on romance than realism. At least it did mean that the place avoided the impression of a 'theme park' with tame locals performing for the edification of the tourists.

It was across the town square into the Southern part of the harbour that one found 'the parrot bar' so named after the owner's African Grey, a young female bird with an already impressive vocal repertoire. Nektarios, my beloved taverna owner also had one of these birds, and rather provocatively encouraged me to put my finger through the bars. Love nearly meant me losing my finger, for the parrot duly gripped it in that beak which can crack a brazil nut and would not let go. I spent about 30 seconds worrying before I was released. So in the bar I was more inclined to commune with the bird by whistling and chirping and generally making a vocal fool of myself, though I did occasionally put a finger through to stroke it, on the top of the head, or back of the neck. This bar was famous for its ice cream which only they and the first bar served then. But Anastasia made her own on the premises, as she did superb cakes.

When it came to eating, there were 5 tavernas on the harbour-front in 1999. The oldest, running since 1954, had till shortly before been the domain of a famous local character, now sadly retired through serious illness. I was rather relieved in some ways that he was no longer cooking, for a feature of his cuisine had been the light dusting of ash which used to descend over everything from his ever-present cigarette. His son Petros had taken over, with his wife helping in the kitchen and a particularly energetic Georgian waiter, Gregori, handling front of house, occasionally assisted by the daughters of the family. They had a particularly good menu of local specialities, and always did the catering for the Sunday picnics, making chicken, *briam* (vegetable stew) *gigantes* (giant beans) Greek salad and potato salad in large quantities.

The traditional setting under the trees, strung with lights for evening, was the charm of the next taverna, a family business still run then by the matriarch, whose triplet daughters were on hand to assist. Their meatballs were to die for, and they were the first to offer *Imam* (aubergines baked with onions and tomatoes). It was a handy place to eat while still watching over the office, and so popular with our agents. When a film crew came to make a wartime drama set on Kalkos it was this taverna which was chosen as the 'village taverna' set. The house behind, up the alleyway was painted (only up to a certain height, amusingly) and used for shots of the hero leaving his house. The only problem for me and Jill and Maggie was that the film crew wanted us to maintain absolute silence in the office (only yards away) while they were recording - difficult to do if your phone starts ringing, or if you need to speak to a client. The production assistant was none too polite in admonishing us for these uncontrollable interruptions. But somehow the recording was made.

Next came one of the oldest tavernas, not now run by its owner, but rented by a striking Armenian lady, a glamorous and sexy creature with a fiery nature. Magda's food was good (especially the unusual features of coleslaw and chicken tagliatelle) but the atmosphere and the standards of service could be trying. She seemed to have a permanent chip on her shoulder about people not coming to her restaurant, failing to observe that sometimes she had good nights while others languished unvisited. It was a difficult location as it jutted out further than the others towards the harbour-front and the big jetty, meaning that the children (and the occasional dog) would be playing, usually noisily, right in front of the establishment, in the wide open space. It was a wonder in those days that we did not lose a few children over the edge because, romantically, but not safely, there were no street lights on the jetty area. This meant that there was a great view of the stars, but not of an unfortunate accident at the water's edge, out in the gloom.

The building was a bit of a barren shed with bare bulb lighting and Sally and I were continually sucked into attempts to advise Magda on how to cheer the place up. Sally went as far as to buy in a supply of candle lamps, which could be useful in power cuts but were a way of softening the atmosphere. That people liked it was obvious the night of a power cut, when the place glowed charmingly and people flocked in. But Magda did not have the courage to try turning her lights off and lighting the candles - even once a week - to pursue this unique attraction. In the end, her solution was hanging baskets of yellow flowers, though these could be a hazard if the wind got up. Indeed, I once witnessed a weird scenario in the '*meltemi*' wind, when the gusts can suddenly turn round. Sparks from the grill at Magda's were swept up by the wind going South then suddenly blown back through the taverna by the wind turning round and going North, blowing them at the unfortunate unsuspecting customers.

Past the centre of the village and the 'parrot bar' was the abode of my dear one, Nektarios. For all my affection for him, I had to admit that his taverna was the weakest on the island, with variable quality. Nektarios was the grill chef, while his sister tried gamely in the main kitchen, and indeed produced the finest octopus in red wine on the island. But one good dish does not make a good taverna. I was a bit annoyed when, having noticed that no one served *hummus* (too Middle Eastern, therefore Turkish, presumably) I offered to make some at home for her to try. She proceeded to dislike it, one of my great specialities. But then, if one is unused to something, and might have resented the implication that one was lacking for not having it on the menu, one would be inclined to be negative about it.

A little further on, one came to the taverna of Petros and his wife Athina. This was the place for the best lamb in roast and chops, while Athina's pumpkin balls (really courgette) were a delightful revelation, and a first for the island. Sadly, both husband and wife were struggling with ill health, Petros with his bad back in particular, and finding the demands of taverna life too much. A problem was voiced which I was to hear from a number of quarters over the years. The sons of the family had no interest in coming into the business. More than almost any other nation, the Greeks work for their children, and it never stops, even into old age. So, of course, what every Greek businessman and woman is hoping for is that the children will take over what they have worked to build up. But the widening of cultural exposure and the opening of horizons outside island life have lead to many of the children wanting to make a life and a career elsewhere, in other fields like medicine, the law, architecture. Or many just cannot cope with the small community life, and need to be in Rhodes

There was no sign of that happening in the next restaurant, where the son of the family was assisted by his semi-retired parents. Dimitri's very large size was a bit startling - one does not see very many extremely fat people in the UK - but he was a charming character, very helpful and speaking very good English owing to his Australian Greek connections. This had been an *ouzeri* in its original foundation, with a tradition in excellent *mezedes* (small portion dishes, often of fish, which are designed to accompany *ouzo* or the like). The Greeks (unlike other nations, the British included) are appalled at the idea of drinking alcohol without having some kind of food with it. The *mezedes* had remained good, and unusual, while the contribution by the mother of the family of 'Kalkos pasta' was the forerunner of many imitations in other tavernas of this traditional local dish. It has to be the ultimate comfort food, with tender home made mini pasta strips soaked in a mixture of sweet caramelised onions and butter, with extra cheese (ouch) on top if desired - probably enough calories for three days in one go.

Out of town, at the beach, there was another taverna, and a cantina. It seemed there might have been another taverna, alongside the first, but, according to rumour, the owner of the first engineered it so that 'archaeological remains' were found in the first excavations for the foundations. So, the site became sacrosanct, and his monopoly preserved. Certainly, Marco's food was excellent, including the legendary and spectacularly filling 'special omelette', and his wife and eldest son made up a good team. But they had a mixed blessing in the eccentric French waiter, Jean-Claude, who traumatised customers and staff alike with his brusque manner and forthright demands for tips. Single women were always ignored, unless they actively appealed to the kitchen team, for such a person would tip badly, such was his theory. This made a lot more sense to me once I discovered that Jean-Claude had agreed to work for tips only, but it was still a thorn in Marcos's flesh till his other sons were old enough to help out, and Jean-Claude ejected from his realm.

But despite his machinations, Marcos could do nothing about his competitor the cantina, which admittedly only served such as burgers and ice cream. This was presided over by local lothario Andreas, whom Maggie had pronounced as 'coming with a health warning'. It was not the most comfortable spot, but it made a change, and the view was great. And of course it was much cheaper than the taverna. A great benefit of the cantina was its suitability as a venue for late night noisy parties for the young people. Admittedly, the few people staying in the studios along at the taverna were not best pleased with this, but for most of the village, it was an ideal situation, not too far to travel but far enough out not to disturb most people's rest.

I was later to discover another solution, on a neighbouring island, where the nightclub had been sited in the old deserted village. I wondered if that might ever happen in Kalkos, where the trip up the mountain might well deter many customers. I did wonder why there was no transport to help people with no cars or bikes of their own. It turned out that there had once been a minibus, which seemed to be an old VW camper van. As often happens, the guy running it got fed up or died or moved away, and no one else wanted to do it, so it was now stationed up near the army base, on the way to the helicopter pad, being used as a chicken shed. This meant that anyone wanting transport up the mountain, tour companies included, was dependent on the baker and his truck. This of course was completely unofficial and uninsured, and one had to quietly slip the guy some drachmas for diesel. It was also a bit alarming to contemplate the return journey, having seen the state of the narrow windy road on the way up, when one had observed the baker downing a few *ouzos* with his mates before the return trip.

An unusual feature of the tavernas was the ever-attendant cats, looking for handouts from the visitor's plates. The tavernas frowned on the practise of slipping these creatures titbits, which they claimed (rightly) encouraged them to come back, made the floor of the taverna messy, and discouraged the cats from pursuing their natural prey, the rodents of the island. Unfortunately, there were rather too many members of the feline tribe on the island, and this could lead to some difficult moments. Firstly, there was the alarming experience of cats leaping up at one to try to steal food off one's plate. Secondly, one would find one's house being invaded, if the doors or windows had been left open (often the case because of the heat.)

The third difficulty was rather amusing in the effect it had on the rather 'respectable' middle class British visitors to the island. I observed one night that, alongside the taverna at the end of the harbour, a number of cats had gathered in an open space. It soon became clear that one of them was a female in season, calling the toms, and that the others were a varied crew of the said toms, lining up for their turn. Well, firstly, the British (even the cat breeders) are unaccustomed to such sights, and untutored in the natural behaviour of feral cats. Forming the audience for a session of feline serial bonking was clearly doing nothing for the visitors' digestion, and there were many shocked exclamations. Wickedly, I could not help speculating that the presence of enthusiastic and noisy sexual activity in their midst might be reminding these people that these days were long gone in their own relationships.

CHAPTER 15 - MANAGING THE JOB

Against the background of all the village characters, I was learning the job, and making it my own. Sarah had been right that there was not much guidance as to exactly what to do, beyond certain basic organisational things. This suited my creative streak ideally, for I do better when I can be an individual, not just delivering a prepared package.

The company billed itself as 'a la carte' and I embraced the tailoring to clients which this implied. The company was owned and run by a Greek, and I began to realise that this meant that one sort of made things up as one went along, as the need arose. I began to earn the respect of Jill and Maggie for how I stamped the identity of the company, with what seemed to them very little guidance. It was a little scary that I was alone as the representative and that therefore it could fall on me to sort out a lot more than their luggage collection, boat trip and taxi ride. Phil, who had many more people to deal with, said he admired me for coping with operating alone.

One thing I blundered with was not to realise that I was expected to buy all the produce for the 'welcome packs' from one shop, ie the agent's father-in-law next door. Admittedly, it was good not to have the hassle of doing it oneself, but I wish I had been told before the embarrassment of being pulled up about it. We provided water, tea, coffee, sugar, milk, wine, bread, butter, honey, cheese, condiments, washing up liquid and sponge, a sort of basic starter kit for what were billed as self-catering holidays (though few did much cooking).

I set about improving the villa books, with increased information and illustrations. I had been to test some of the locations myself, for example the walk to the Monastery of St John the Far, far off on a high plateau in the mountains, almost at the other, Western, end of the island. This was the last outing for the famous pink walking boots which had carried me up to the *Kalivia* to meet Nelly the dog and Elsie. They were soon to fall victim to the curious phenomenon (unknown to a Briton) of rubber items literally crumbling away because of heat. Even although it was still early in the season, the end of May, and early in the morning when I started, I was soon very hot, and got sunburnt, having taken inadequate precautions. I ended up making a whole day of it, with a climb of two and a quarter hours to get to the Monastery, and a quick wander round. Always one to attempt too much, I made my return to the village via a beach down a seemingly interminable zigzag track. Tiny, with white pebbles, and rather active waves, it was an exciting spot. I attempted a swim, glad to have had personal experience of the power of the water here, so able to warn of the currents. Thinking back on the expedition, and remembering that I had no phone in those days, I was glad that I had at least told the agency what I was doing, as indeed we liked clients to do if they were going off walking. Ironically, back then, the mobile phone coverage was not nearly so good, rendering such a 'safety net' useless, and even years later the mountains could soon interfere with reception.

I collected lots of dried flower heads, thistles, grasses, impressed with how well-preserved they were, lacking the mushy quality of old vegetation in the UK. Bearing these treasures, I finally stumbled into the cantina at the beach for some refreshment. Here I was served by Andreas, in his thirties, but still one of the biggest *kamaki* on the island (he of Maggie's 'health warning'). He was certainly tall dark and handsome and obviously keen to impress a new lady, charmingly insisting on wrapping up my dried treasures in a foil bouquet. I was less impressed with the ice cream lolly however, which was so runny that I was instantly spattered, and had to resort to a plate and a spoon. Obviously, his poor freezer was fighting a losing battle against its over-exposed position in the heat.

Another expedition I undertook was to the windmills, with their stone and woodwork restored but no sails in place. There was no real clear path to the windmills, but just a kind of stony goat track off the army road to the helicopter pad. I looked at all three from the outside, but only found one with the door unlocked. My planned exploration of the interior was truncated suddenly by the sad and revolting discovery of a dead sheep on the floor. Obviously, it had wandered in and found the door slammed by the wind behind it, leaving it to die of thirst. And the wind was very strong that day as it happened. I had been intrigued by the sight of something flapping up on the red-coloured roof of the middle windmill. When I got closer, I was alarmed to find it was sheet metal, flapping like cloth in the gusts. A quick inspection of the ground revealed a number of large pieces scattered about, all of which could have made a nasty mess of anyone in range when they were flying around. I glanced nervously at the large piece which was threatening to tear off, and made a swift retreat.

If I had escaped injury that day, one of my clients was not so lucky. About a month into the job, I had a tiny Irish lady staying at a small apartment. One day, she went to one of the public swimming points on the North side of the harbour, in amongst the terraces of various sea-front villas. She had taken with her a rush beach mat to lie on, but made the mistake of stepping on it, whereupon it slid away from her. She fell on her wrist and broke it. Luckily, the people at the next door villa were in and heard her cries. And someone came to the office to fetch me. Meanwhile, Fivos the young doctor had been summoned. He did a good job of temporarily strapping and administering pain killers, while I made plans to take us both to the hospital in Rhodes the following morning. There, an x-ray was taken, and an attempt to set the arm made. We returned to Kalkos that afternoon, she by now in a cast and a sling. As it happened (wrists being very difficult things to set) she had to have it operated on back home - and sent me the photographs, rather gruesome ones featuring pins on a frame.

But she was to suffer a hardship on top of the pain and inconvenience of her injured wrist. To this day, I still find it incredible that what is supposed to be a human being could have behaved like this. The villain of the piece was none other than the annoying philandering fisherman whom I had had to get rid of during my first week. It seems he had turned his attention to my client, and, seeming not to understand a refusal, had tried to force his way inside her apartment. Well,

I realise these guys think foreign women are easy prey but what satisfaction could there be, what *kudos*, for him in taking advantage of a tiny, injured woman? It marked him as both cruel and pathetic. But worse was to come, for when I told his friend, my amour Nektarios, how disgusted I was, Nektarios was most put out with me, probably because I had had the nerve to criticise the behaviour of that 'god on earth' figure, a Greek male.

One useful side benefit of the accident was that I grew in the admiration of my co-workers in the agency, notably Kostas, that rather grumpy character who was never too pleased when I complained over the dreadful old fax machine which often frustrated me, especially when I had to reload its paper roll. It seems amazing, looking back now, how primitive our technology was when after only a few years we have now got wireless internet connections.

I had also gained some popularity for throwing myself into sorting out the library of books which crowded the shelves around the room. Here, once more, one had to beware of Kosta's ridiculously protective attitude to 'his' books. It seemed he had had a donation a few years previously, and had carefully stamped the agency name inside all the volumes. Now we used to let people take books they were interested in, and often they would return fresh ones they had finished with. In the opinion of us 'reps' this was a good thing, but Kostas (no librarian, he) could never come to terms with people going off with 'his' books, failing of course to notice that they were giving him new ones to replace them. It also failed to occur to him (and he is still like this) that if everyone returned all the books and also left us new ones, there would quickly be no room in the office for any people, desks, computers, etc, only books. My greatest triumph was to get away with sorting the books for quality at the very beginning and somehow managing to throw away those which were (a) in dire condition (b) of appalling literary quality. Somehow Kosta's antennae failed to pick up what I was doing, or maybe, for once, he decided to trade off his displeasure against the undoubted benefits of having me grafting away so hard, meaning he did not have to.

Although it was useful for helping me learn some Greek, sitting in the office listening to Greeks relating to each other could be quite emotionally stressful. It is hard for a more reserved race like the British to grasp that these people can be screaming in apparent hatred one minute and then suddenly shaking hands, wreathed in smiles. 'Full and frank discussion' is surely a concept invented in Greece. I just could not cope in the early days, and used to flee the office, heart pounding, to let them get on with it.

One of the things for which I was very dependent on the agents, of course, was the matter of maintenance on the properties, for communication with most of the people who could mend things or supply services were Greek speakers only. I quickly realised that it was useless to expect UK standards of finish and maintenance on a small island with little or no infrastructure in terms of spare parts. It was the land of the 'bodger'. And the trouble is, once you have bodged, you have to bodge again, for the joint you constructed will not now admit a genuine part. It is understandable of course that people became adept at doing this, living where they did, for they had to be resourceful for things to be kept working at all.

What did make me cringe, however, was that the

owners would expect to get away with pitiful standards when it came to the age of the mattresses and pillows, the quality and quantity of crockery and cutlery, the paucity of cooking facilities, the grottiness or absence of outside furniture. I spent a lot of money over the years trying to alleviate this sort of thing. It was probably my early efforts which alerted the company accountant Simeon to regard me with some suspicion. But it was up to him to recoup the expense from the owners.

Thankfully, my clients were a very charming lot, often busy top professionals grabbing a quick break in a quiet spot. One couple used to say that they came on holiday to talk to each other, for they never found the time, hardly seeing each other at home. Others would lug over every book they had wanted to read for the past year, causing our luggage delivery man to grunt and strain. Then they would just sit on the sunny terrace catching up. Of course, the readers of the island, and our friend Kostas, would eventually benefit from this heavy luggage. I used to give them all lots of information, in written form and on my visits, but I was always careful to point out that there was no pressure to do anything; we just did not want them to miss out on what there was, if they wanted it.

But the only time I broke my rule about 'selling' was one week when the picnic to the neighbouring deserted island was going to fail to run because the numbers were insufficient. Jill and Maggie's company had not produced enough so it was down to me and my clients. There was a family of seven staying at a large old villa, who had expressed a reasonable interest in going, but were inclined to leave it for the following week. I rushed up there, explained the situation, notably stressing that they could see it was possible they might miss the chance altogether the next week, so they signed up. I returned in triumph to the office, and a great time was had by all.

This family were the centre of the worst flight delay I ever had to deal with as a representative, on the 23rd of June, a month into my job. It was ultimately the fault of a light aircraft which was bringing executives from a mobile phone company to Rhodes. This plane crashed on the runway, and instead of clearing it away, the authorities closed the airport for hours so there could be an assessment. This meant planes being diverted to Crete and Kos. The family, Mum, Dad three children and the wife's parents were scheduled to take off from Rhodes about 1.30pm. But the diversion of the planes had had a knock on effect. The pilot only had enough flying hours left to bring the plane in, about four hours late. We then had to wait for another crew to come out in order to take the aircraft and over 300 passengers home. I dread to think how much all this cost the airline, for delays of certain numbers of hours mean that all passengers have to be fed. The airline did us proud, hiring a lovely large club on the outskirts of the next village North of the airport, and taking us there by coach for a marvellous spaghetti and salad buffet. I was nearly running out of steam in the charm department, and had a vicious stress headache. But finally we got back to the airport, and, about 10pm, I waved the family goodbye and started contemplating a night in a Rhodes hotel.

I had been lucky that day, in that I had had no one arriving off the dreaded delayed flight, for I would have had to find rooms for them. But, amazingly, when I phoned Kosta's mobile to report a safe departure at last, my luck continued.

'Get down to the port now Frances!' cried Kostas, 'There's a late charter!'

Lucky again, I found a willing taxi driver and we zoomed through the night. And indeed, just as we got to the quay, the boat was pulling in, and who should be getting off but Kostas himself, taking his grandson back to Rhodes. This was the smaller of the two local boats, and my preferred one, though there was not a lot to choose between the two sets of crusty old boatmen. But for the first time I saw Yiannis smile, as he came to me, the lone passenger, to collect my fare.

I was standing at the very front of the main deck, with the sea and sky open before me, black and glittering silver in a glorious full moon. I felt like a queen in her chariot, riding high, and yet dazzled, awed by this eerie beauty.

'*Oreia, nai?*' grinned Yiannis, clearly appreciating the beauty, but somehow failing to find the poetry in the moment. I felt a stab of envy, and an understanding of how these guys could put up with the job day after day.

When we reached the harbour, I saw Nektarios moving around near the taverna and experienced a stab of hope that he was going to come and meet me off the boat. Obviously, I had had an overdose of romance during the voyage which had given me unrealistic expectations of my loved one, who was actually engaged in transporting bottles of water to the taverna. One of my weaknesses with men is to construct too much of a relationship out of not very much, and of course my expectations only rebound to hurt me.

I had already coped with a client being injured in resort, but now my boss was asking if I could cope with someone coming who had broken his leg, but did not want to cancel his booking. Well, it would depend on which house he was booked to stay in, some of them being high in the village, with lots of steps. As luck would have it, he was in the central one, which was possible to get to mostly 'on the flat' with only a few steps up to the house itself. I was nervous about meeting him and had to rearrange the taxis to allow him more leg room. But he turned out to be a very brave indomitable character, with a supportive wife and family, who managed to get around surprisingly well on his crutches.

Two encounters early on defined my character in the job. Firstly, Simeon, the company accountant, came to stay. I had to put him in our least appealing apartment, as it was vacant. Simeon had seemed a bit suspicious of me, as if he thought I was out to get more than my due out of the company. I was therefore anxious to please. He told me he had no shower gel, so I galloped off to the supermarket. But by the time I got back, he had been in the shower, and I was confronted with this decidedly attractive man clad only in a small towel round his waist. It was even more embarrassing to be sitting there discussing company matters in these provocative circumstances. I decided, however, that I was being tested, in the area of my moral rectitude. Pleased though he might have been for his own vanity if I had made a pass at him, he no doubt would have considered me untrustworthy as a representative. The company had been unlucky with their employees on other islands, one turning out to be a sex fiend who took her conquests to bed in the house she was borrowing from her boss, and another a drunk who had to be fished out of the ditch into which she had fallen while lurching her way home. Well, whatever Simeon's real agenda was, I passed that test.

However with one of my early clients I indulged the adventurous side of my character too much. This guy, Peter, was with us for 2 weeks in a very nice upstairs apartment. During the first week, he was the perfect intellectual holidaymaker, occupying himself with walking, reading and painting watercolours. Then he met the graphic designer from Essex and her mates, staying in a big seafront villa; and turned into 'Essex boy' overnight, getting into late night partying and skinny dipping. Included in the gang, I came along for this last expedition, which we managed with surprising modesty considering we had only one towel among us, passed down the beach like a relay baton. I had one of my amazingly lucky experiences - though the luck was not really mine - when, emerging from the water in just the right spot, I looked down to see something glinting in the sand, caught in the faint light of a half moon. I scooped it up, to find it was a silver and pearl earring, and luckily, delving next to it, found its partner, about to be lost forever below the surface. Once a bit more decent, I showed off my find, to be met with a delighted shriek from the graphic designer. Unbelievably, utterly fecklessly, she had taken the earrings off and just laid them on the sand (!) when entering the water. Worse, they were not even her earrings, but borrowed from a friend. Well, 'There's nowt so queer as folk!' goes the old saying.

Despite my triumph, the smile was about to be wiped off my face by Peter, who decided to tease me that I would be out of a job when he told the holiday company what I had been getting up to.

'You're not really their sort, are you?'

Then, to my dismayed countenance, he twinkled,

'Far too lively and daring!'

We retreated into more respectable activities after that, but it taught me never to assume anything about people's potential from what can appear to be their usual behaviour. However, none of my trials and successes could have prepared me for the strange behaviour and dramatic events of a hot night in early July.

CHAPTER 16 - STRANGER IN THE NIGHT

'Hardly working!' said the visitors from the UK, consumed with envy that their company's representatives should be able to enjoy the island of Kalkos for the whole summer, with, according to them, no real job to do. Yes, it was a paradise island in many ways and not the sort of travel rep's job familiar to viewers of documentaries set in the sleazier parts of Ibiza or Faliraki. Most of Kalkos's visitors – at least in outward impression – were respectable middle-aged couples. But, as Jean Paul Sartre said, 'Hell is other people'. Foibles too fantastic to report were the agents' and reps' daily diet as the holiday spirit liberated the darker reaches of the clients' psyches. But for me, the most amazing events took place on a night in early July 1999, transfer day for the island.

One look at him told his reps that he was not a typical client. For a start, he was young, athletic, but adding the earring and the (arty not nautical) tattoos marked him out as potential trouble. Further evidence for this was his non-appearance at the transfer coach. Add his preference for taking a lift (and whatever illegal substances were also on offer) from our chief local reprobate and his trouble rating moved up towards the red. I made a mental note of relief that he was not with my company.

Peace reigned temporarily during the boat trip and the show-in to villas, but it was not long before Phil and Sally, the representatives, heard from him and his girlfriend. Apparently their apartment was crawling with cockroaches (estimate 34!). Although immediate inspection merely produced 2 dead ones, it seemed prudent to placate the couple by moving them elsewhere. All seemed well. The companies' reps sat over a bottle of Metaxa talking over the day, unloading the stress till feeling able to sleep at gone 2.00am.

It was a hot night (no surprise in a Greek July) and I had the windows and shutters open in my little apartment, windows which were large and near to the ground. The curtains were tied together to prevent any wind destroying my privacy in the bedroom at the end, and in the living room in the middle. My kitchen and bathroom both led off the other end. Not long into my sleep, the suspect client was beginning an adventure…

…but I first became aware of it at about 3.45 when I was awakened by a voice at the bedroom window.

'Are you all right? I should shut your windows if I were you!'

in a West Country accent, as had my male fellow rep. What the devil was Phil doing coming round to check on me? I had only left his house 2 hours before. So I thought, as I got up and put my robe on. Pushing the curtains aside, I looked out - nothing. But then, just as I was about to turn away, I saw a male figure, apparently clad in a bathing suit, coming down the stone steps opposite my door. I decided he must be on his way to the nearby public swimming place. It was a funny time to do it, but it was hot and it was a free country. Reassured, I slipped off my robe, and attempted the return to bed.

I never got there, for the voice spoke again. And I could not make out the words, for now I was scared. But I had to look, so I pushed the curtains out again and was startled to see a young man (in profile) standing outside – most definitely NOT in the bathing suit I thought I had seen. Now there were unkind souls among my circle who suggested that my likely reaction to an attractive stark-naked (rather well-endowed actually) young man within grabbing range would have been to haul him in over the window ledge. Not so! For once, Fearless Fran betrayed her nickname.

Clutching my robe I retreated fast to the living room, watching the bedroom the while, chilled to see a hand s l o w l y push the curtains inwards. While nerves made me grope for my fags, another ghastly thought intruded. The door shutters were open, the door only on the latch! Surely it was my guardian angel who helped my frantic hand find my keys in the dark - and the right one for the lock - even as I saw 'the hand' pushing the living room curtains s l o w l y inwards. Cowering in the entrance to the bathroom, smoking about 3 fags at once, I expected my visitor to attempt a climb in over one of the window ledges (no trouble to a fit young man). But then, at the height of my panic, I became aware of a commotion along the street – angry voices, the word 'police'. Ah, thank goodness, the police are here, thought I. Well, not exactly. The commotion went on. After a couple of minutes I gingerly opened the door. There, on my doorstep, stick in hand, was Manolis from one of the bars, not interested in me or my house, but studying intently the house across the way, next to the steps opposite.

'Aargh, Manoli!' I exclaimed, 'There's a naked man trying to get into my house!'

'Don't worry. We are here. Go back to sleep!' he urged, optimistically.

'Go back to sleep!? With you lot making all this racket?!'

I closed the door, but stayed behind it, listening. It was entertaining stuff.

Dramatis personae:-

Naked Man (henceforward referred to as N.M.)

Local gang members (individual identities unknown, referred to as 'gang')

Girl - occupant of house opposite (a non-speaking role)

Myself in a thinking role (F)

Location:-

patio of house, outside toilet of house, *Frances in her house.*

(*from inside toilet*) N.M: I want some clothes

(*on patio*) Gang: Why did you leave the house without them?

N. M.: My toilet was blocked. I was looking for a toilet.

Gang: Why did you come here?

N. M.: I thought this was a public toilet

F: Wow, nice for the girl who lives there!

Gang: Come out so that we can help you.

N. M.: I'm not coming out 'cos you'll beat me up

F: He's got a point there....

Gang: It's all right we won't hurt you. We are all going to the police.

N. M.: I don't know. I don't trust....

Gang: Come out.

N. M.: I can't. I have no clothes.

Girl; *(obviously anxious to be rid of this encumbrance)* *brings small towel to gang members*

Gang: You can't stay here. We have a towel you can put on.

N. M.: I don't want to go to the police. I don't want to come out. You will hurt me.

Gang: We can call the police to come here, or you can come with us.

And so on for another set of exchanges until finally...

Gang: Here put this on.

(emerging from toilet now with small towel round waist) N. M.: I don't want to go to the police. What about my girlfriend?

More exchanges, inaudible to me, as the gang and captive proceed down the street to the police station.

Peace reigned in the street but not in my nervous system. No way could I have slept even with the chance, but, soon after, I found myself comforting Sally, the female member of the rep team who had charge of this unusually 'difficult' client. It was she who filled me in on his earlier adventures, and told me the sequel.

Marcos, the Mayor's brother had been asleep in his little house on the first level up from the harbour. His greatest difficulty was having no hands (lost in a fishing accident) and at that time he was still waiting for his prosthetics.

Some time around 3.00 his sleep was interrupted by the arrival of our naked friend (his first visit of the night). Poor

Marcos, shocked by awakening to the sight of a naked man in his house, and ill-equipped to defend himself, cried out, and his visitor fled. Marcos wasted no time in shooting off down to Manoli's bar, where, despite the late hour, a small company still remained – but not including Manolis himself. He was on a visit to his father-in-law Michalis, boss of the Hotel, over at the other end of the harbour. Marco's frantic tale of his intruder was greeted with amused incredulity by the late night drinkers, and he lapsed into a sulk.

But vindication was just around the corner for, with extraordinarily poor judgement, the naked man chose the Hotel for his next exploits. To say that Michali's temper was ballistic was putting it mildly and it is a wonder that a shotgun does not feature prominently in the night's events. The hapless occupants of 2 rooms (in one a mother and her baby) paid for their open patio windows with the terror of the 'naked invasion', before Michalis and cohorts were alerted and the intruder fled. But now Manolis was on the case, and set off post haste for his bar to summon a 'search party'.

Needless to say, the sulking Marcos was delighted to have his story confirmed. Through him, his brother Alexandros the Mayor was aroused. As luck would have it, Alexandros was the agent for the travel company, able to access the villa and to alert the reps. So a two-pronged assault on the situation began, with the gang in pursuit of the offender, and Alexandros off to visit the villa and the girlfriend.

While our naked friend was attempting to get into my villa, Alexandros had entered his, to find the girlfriend spark out on the bed, fully clothed, presumably after 'drink taken' (Ouzo on an empty stomach was implicated as a guilty party throughout this adventure.) Lucky it was that Sally witnessed the ensuing events. The girlfriend, suddenly awoken, still drink-fuddled, thought the male figure was her boyfriend and attempted to embrace him. Alexandros resisted, and later commented, (with actions)

'She want me, but I push her away. Many women want me, but I push them away!' (reversing the habits of a lifetime...)

Alexandros asked

'Why has your husband no dresses? Give me dresses for your husband!' The poor girlfriend, fazed, gasped,

'But he's never done anything like this before!'

Eventually, groggily, she assembled a t-shirt and shorts combo with which the company departed for the police station. Though surrounded by police and the gang members, the unclothed one displayed a remarkable level of confidence, possibly buoyed up by the arrival of his girlfriend. Confronted with the once-longed-for clothes he exclaimed,

'I don't need those...I don't even need this!' whipping off the little towel and strutting round the police station 'in the buff'.

Oh, how the Greek guys relished the opportunity to scrutinise and criticise a foreign male! The general opinion (naturally) was that he had nothing worthy of display anyway. Sorry guys, beg to differ, I smirked to myself when I heard this.

Commonsense intervened in the shape of Phil the traumatised rep, who got the fellow dressed and back to his villa to be kept under guard till departure on the early boat (hand-cuffed to a stanchion for maximum dramatic effect). On the neighbouring large island of Rhodes he would be charged with 'disturbing public peace' or such offence. Unbelievably, for once, the Greek courts worked like lightning, and the wretched offender, displaying his by now familiar lack of judgement, paid his (large) fine and returned to the small island on the early afternoon boat. Horror-struck, Phil had to confide in him that, were he to stay, he would be 'filled in', and then had to get up early again to escort the couple to Rhodes to finish their holiday in another resort. I happened to be on that boat, for a shopping trip on my day off. A dancer it seems, elegant, apparently sane, there was the creature who had sent an exquisite 'frisson' of scandalised horror through a community now falling over itself to dine out on the story. To my shame, I was to regret that my 'bottle' failed over the impulse to sidle up to him and whisper in his 'shell-like', 'Nice dick!'

CHAPTER 17 - BOATS AND BUGS

Nothing as thrilling as the 'naked man' incident occurred again that Summer, but nevertheless I continued to have all sorts of fun by night and day, on land and sea.

I did find the heat very oppressive (hence the open windows and shutters), and was to pay for this one night after returning (full of Metaxa) from an outing. Suddenly, in through the window came a very large and thoroughly recognisable insect, a revolting, leggy, caramel coloured flying cockroach. Well, a sober Fran would have shrieked in terror and spent the next 2 hours fiddling about trying to catch the thing, fearful of killing it because of the crunching noise, the mess (and what I had been told was the horrible smell the corpse would release). However, Metaxa-filled Fran lunged with the speed of light and crushed the still disorientated insect under my sandal, then, trying not to look, scraped up the remains in some toilet paper. If there was a smell, I didn't notice, but then I have always been a bit deficient in that sense (leading to a lurking fear that my house is smelly to outsiders, unbeknown to me).

Certainly one smell with which one became familiar was that of cockroach and ant spray. This was strong stuff and our advice to visitors was to give the place a thorough spraying just before rushing out the door, leaving it to do its work and subside before one's return. I always put sprays automatically in all our accommodations, which saved running around supplying them or assisting in their purchase individually. But one of the things tourists had to buy for themselves was ant powder, which rejoiced in what was, for the British, the gloriously embarrassing name of 'Pubex'. Of course in Greek this would be pronounced with an 'r' sound at the beginning, and have no strange connotations that one was buying something to rid oneself of 'crabs'.

But the bug that had got me was the 'skinny-dipping' one. I would go off by myself for such exploits, sometimes to the sandy beach, but on one occasion to the rocky coves round the headland from the Hotel. That particular night, I was put off my daring pursuit, for, as I splashed in the shallows, I heard the puttering of a fishing boat engine getting closer, and ended up crouched among the rocks, in a panic in case they intended to make landfall in the cove. Thankfully they chugged on past, but I decided that such tension about discovery was not worth it when the swimming was supposed to be relaxing.

So I contented myself with late night visits to the sandy beach to lie on the sun-beds and look up at the stars. It truly was awesome how many could be seen. The more one looked, the more the background of velvet black revealed itself as containing further myriads of tiny pinpricks, unimaginably far away. I only wished I knew more about the stars and planets. The fount of knowledge on this was Phil, whose interest must have begun in the Navy. This was about the one topic on which you could rely on him to talk seriously, for usually he was a 'wind-up' merchant, which could actually be quite trying.

On the nights when the moon was at or near the full, I would attempt a moonlight watercolour painting. I did one of the Hotel, from outside Nektario's taverna, and several of the bay at the beach, from the taverna. Even more than on Stargos, I was struck with the incredible illuminating power of the Moon when not in competition with too many yellow tinged street lights. The most remarkable was the strength of the shadows cast by oneself and other objects. And then there was the Moon itself, the *fengari* much celebrated in Greek song. We were continually surprised with its sheer size, and where it came up, but even more delighted by its rising display of fabulous blood orange colours.

Naturally, on an island, boats of all sorts feature very prominently in everyone's life, from those admiring elegant yachts through binoculars, to the fishermen struggling to eke a living from a diminishing fish stock, in the face of increased Government taxes, to the skilled captain of the huge inter-island ferry manoeuvring in the bay. And then there was me, hankering after a boat but accepting my complete cluelessness - and knowing that I would have to choose between a boat and my car (far more user-friendly).

I did have some interesting encounters with boats during my first year on Kalkos. First of all, there was the trip to Trachea, on the little fishing boat which had belonged to Jill's deceased husband, now run for private trips by her brother in law Andreas. I had arranged for this trip with him to happen on my day off so I had no choice but to go. The trouble was that I had one of the worst hangovers I have ever had, and despite the water I had brought, my headache became truly

awesome. Again, I could not escape from my torment, for Alex would deliver one to the beach (inaccessible by foot) and return quite a number of hours later to pick one up. So I was stuck, luckily in the shade of cliffs undercut by erosion, on the Eastern beach of what was the neck of a virtual island off the south coast of Kalkos. My mission had been to do a painting of the scene, so I set to. And amazingly, despite my debilitated sensibilities, I produced what I considered at the time to be one of my finest watercolours yet. That I have never sold it yet in my gallery I attribute to the fact that there is no sky in the picture only the cliffs opposite my beach position. But I learned a lot about painting, even if not necessarily about abstaining from drinking.

Our normal boat service left at 06.00 and got to the little harbour on Rhodes at 07.15, which left just enough time to get the bus to the main harbour in the North, where a boat to Symi could be caught. I went to visit my colleague, but could only spare one day, so I had an exhausting journey starting at 06.00 (up at 05.00 of course) then on the boat to Symi at 09.00, arriving after 11.00, and immediately touring the company's properties, and the agency, with my Symi colleague Jackie, before collapsing for a boozy lunch and somnolent afternoon. I could not stay out late at dinner, for I had to be back on the boat at 07.00 the next morning in order to catch the 14.30 from the little harbour to get back to Kalkos: a huge amount of travelling for not too much time seeing the other island. But it was worth it. Symi is spectacular, breathtaking. That harbour with its ice cream houses piled up on impossible slopes is one of the wonders and treasures of the world. Not for nothing does it attract the rich and famous eg Tom Cruise and Nicole Kidman on their yacht, but it has been spoiled for many by the continual influx of many day-trippers, and the increased traffic and noise on the harbour-front. Kalkos was picking up more and more ex-Symi fans looking for the old quieter days.

The direct connection between these two islands (not that far apart geographically) had been abandoned about 5 years before, after the inter-island ferry service stopped. Sometimes, we would have hydrofoils operating which cut the journey to Symi from Rhodes down to 45 minutes from 2 hours and the journey from Rhodes to Kalkos down to 75 minutes from the main harbour, rather than the same after an hour's drive down the island. This was especially useful when I had clients who were on 2-centre holidays, one week on Kalkos and one on Symi.

Although the visitors tended to call the excursion to our deserted neighbouring island of Alimnia 'the boat trip', the main event of the day was the picnic, which was really a full buffet meal transported to be served on portable tables. That we carried roast chicken, *briam* (vegetable stew), *gigantes* (giant baked beans) *horiatiki* (Greek salad) and potato salad was a strain on our nerves, for occasionally there could be accidents getting into the rowing boat from the ship, or out of it onto the shore. More than once, the fish got a superb lunch of *gigantes* or *briam* (thankfully never the chicken!) as the pot either fell in or slopped over. Luckily, our guests were only to glad to help carry food and cool boxes of drink up the beach to the shade of the trees where we set up the serving area. Drink was restricted to retsina, lemonade and water in those days.

Within a few minutes, we would have the 'bar' open, and one of us would be on duty there while the others dressed the salads, cut the bread and set out the knives and forks, plates, serving spoons and so on. It was always difficult dressing the potato salad, for the dish was inevitably only just big enough to hold the potato, which made mixing in the salt and pepper and mayonnaise a bit tricky, without a spare container. The Greek salad was served with the *feta* cheese separate, as some people did not like it, or it would get too messy, and unevenly shared if all mixed in. Once all that was done, we would ring the 'signal' goat bell, and a queue would start to form, with the temporary canteen staff all busy doling out their respective dishes. We did have to have a word with our Greek helper, Helen's delightful mother Maria, who would insist on saying to people, 'Have you got your fork 'n knife?' a phrase fraught with peril in its spoken form. Finally, all would be served and the 'staff' got their lunch, sitting on the cool boxes.

Somehow, the washing up became my job, dragging the crate of plates down to the sea for a preliminary rinse, always attracting shoals of little darting fish eager to grab some scraps. In those days, the leftovers were given to the local goats, of which the boldest would be lurking nearby. One family of boatmen had been born on this island, and still had animals there, so they would occupy themselves with tending to them, or visiting their former house or church, while we held the picnic.

Up at the village, apart from the old taverna where the boat graffiti were found, there was a charming little church, and a number of houses in various stages of falling down. The other church was on the point between the two bays, near the ruined First World War barracks. Traditionally, this church dedicated to St George was the scene of festivities on April 23rd, St George's Day, when much of the village on Kalkos would come over on the boat.

Another intriguing feature was the 'salt flats' which lay at the head of the bay, just below the village. This must have been a deliberate construction, from which the islanders had been able to make salt, that necessity of life. Looking up to the highest point of Alimnia (far less mountainous than Kalkos) one could see a small Knights of St John castle. This was indeed part of the chain of castles where the garrisons could signal to each other with fire, usually to warn of pirates, who abounded in the region for hundreds of years. Kritinia on Rhodes, Alimnia, then Kalkos, could pass the signal on.

Getting people back to the boat could be a difficult

matter, for although in those days we were still allowed to swim back, there were many who did not want to, or some such as young children (or my elderly father) who could not. This required us to stabilise the small boat while people climbed in, 9 at a time, to be ferried across and then helped by the strong arms of the boatmen to climb up onto the tail-gate of the *kaiki*. That he coped with this at all makes me realise how much fitter my father was back then. Of course my sons had already swum back and were able to give assistance with Dad. On this trip, I was able to observe at close hand the technique of standing up rowing, where the boatman does not scull as we are accustomed to see, back towards where he is going, but stands facing the direction of travel. This means a different motion in pushing and pulling the oars, as the forward pull to move the boat comes from raising the handles and pushing them away to get the nearly vertical blades to bite on the water, then lowering the handles and pulling back to clear the blades from the water and put them in position to pull again. (I had to draw myself a diagram to check all this out.) In other words it is basically the same motion of the blades, but the operator is pushing on the oars where he would normally be pulling, and vice versa. The advantage of being able to see more is surely outweighed, however, by the difficulty of remaining stable while standing up in the boat. Try this is ultra-calm waters only!

Another testing trip, in a different way, was the evening I went on the round the island boat trip on the larger of our 2 *kaikis*. Now this boat was then relatively new and (somewhat embarrassingly) built in Turkey, memories still fresh of her predecessor, a wooden vessel now moored up in Alimnia. But the boat's reputation was as under-ballasted, a bit top heavy and thus inclined to roll more than most. We set off on a beautiful late August evening, Eastwards out of Emborio, then turning Northwards to proceed along that coastline. The trouble always is that in Kalkos the harbour and the South can seem quite calm, but where the sea rolls in from the unprotected North conditions can be much rougher. The sea indeed got lively as we ploughed on westwards, I on the top deck doing rep duty with the people up there, and nearly sliding from my seat. My drink can rolled away never to be retrieved. This was moving from thrilling to scary. But things got worse as we neared the Western tip of the island, where currents met. Now the boat was bucking and plunging in a most alarming manner, and there was a heart-stopping moment when she seemed to hang suspended but threatened between all the forces working on her.

Thank goodness that Maggie, a very experienced sailor with her master's certificate, waited till much later to tell me that that moment represented a yaw and a something and a something else all happening together and she knew that the captain had only seconds to do something restorative before we would capsize. Well luckily he did the right thing and we got round the point into calmer waters with the sunset and a brush with disaster behind us. It is interesting to realise that on only two subsequent occasions has the boat ever gone all round the island. Usually, they confine themselves to visiting beaches and then returning by the same route. That experience at the Western tip may well have been repeated and the good will of Poseidon tested enough, I reckon.

CHAPTER 18 - FAMILY VISIT

My father and sons once again came to see me in my new country, this time taking advantage of a good deal from the company for a house in the middle of the village. This was a lovely traditional house, with 2 bedrooms, a big kitchen living room, a bath (half size) in the bathroom and, very ground-breaking, air-conditioning. It was August, and very hot, so the latter was very welcome.

I was still living in my little house, though the money which I was about to receive from my aunt's estate had encouraged me to look at a property over near the church, and put in an offer for it. This had, to my dismay, been rejected as someone else, an artist who frequented the island, had apparently expressed an interest. But the property-buying impetus was there, now pent up. One day, my father and I were walking along the harbour-front and I looked up at a big house on the next level up, which had a 'for sale' notice on it 'poletai'.

'Gosh that looks nice, I think we should go and see it,' said I.

'Well, I'm happy to have a look. See what you can find

out,' replied Dad.

That evening, on duty in the office, I looked across the room and was puzzled but pleasantly surprised to see what appeared to be an estate agent's advertising poster for the very house, displayed over the agent's desk. This was unheard of in Kalkos, where houses were bought and sold by word of mouth, and little was publicly known of what was actually for sale. It turned out that, because these people were friends of the agent, and lived in Thessaloniki, a long way to travel, she had agreed to handle the sale for them.

'Helen, I am really interested in that house. I would like to see it.'

Taken aback, Helen looked at me.

'Seriously?

'Yes indeed. Dad and I want to look at it.'

'Ok. I'll speak to the owner and arrange something.'

So it was, the next evening, Helen took us up to the mansion, to meet the owner, a very pleasant lady of Kalkos descent who spoke no English, and her charming husband, a retired vet. The house was in her name, inherited from her family, but of less use now she had moved to her second husband's area. We found out later that it had been for sale for a while but that they kept dithering about whether to sell all of it or part of it, if divided into upstairs and downstairs apartments. Many people had looked at it and considered it, notably our eventual 'front-wards' neighbours, and the founder and then boss of one of the local villa holiday companies.

The downstairs of the house contained a largish square hall, with double doors at the front off the patio, and similar off a side passage. The kitchen was at the back left, with a double bedroom to the right. A single bedroom and the bathroom faced each other to left and right of the hall. There was a side passage, and a small back terrace, looking down into the kitchen because of the slope of the land. Extensive, impressive and in good condition, with all the furniture and equipment like cutlery, pots and pans etc included, it seemed a very good deal.

Dad and I then found the only real drawback of the house - a very steep and tricky staircase which ascended like a ladder from just inside the front door. We had barely recovered from pondering the implications of having to continually tackle this when we were bowled over by the stunning spectacle of the painted ceiling, to which the photos had failed to do justice. After a quick tour of the two bedrooms with their double built in platform beds, and the shower room, at present being refurbished, we were ushered onto the balcony. If we liked the house before, we were now in love. The view was amazing - almost the whole sweep of the harbour-front, down the coast of Rhodes, and over to the deserted island. This had been the house of the Turkish governor, built in the 19th Century, and one could see why he had chosen it. It was tall, beautiful, in a commanding position.

While a bit of discussion was going on among the Greeks, Dad and I had a *sotto voce* conversation.

'I want to stay here for the rest of my life, ' he announced, rather startlingly.

'Dad we've got to buy this house!'

And so a momentous decision came upon us, fated to be. For the house was waiting for us, I am sure, and we were, in our separate ways, about to receive the money to

share in a bold and glorious investment. Helen was urging us not to show too much enthusiasm but though we held back a bit verbally, we could hardly conceal the excitement we felt at having such an opportunity within our grasp.

Basically, the couple fell in love with us, especially with my delightful father. And once Greeks like you, you have gone a long way. We soon acquired a helper, who had at one time purchased the little house in front which had been part of the big property in the past. In fact, it had been the kitchen block and servants' quarters, adjoining a small courtyard garden. Sadly, this man had cut down the magnificent old tree which had shaded the yard, saying that it attracted insects. Notwithstanding our resentment about that, it was wonderful to have a bilingual helper, smoothing over the various meetings to do with pre-contracts and so on. Strangely, although we would have been proceeding down an ultra-cautious route as usual in the UK, in Greece we just went for it without a thought of how sound the house was (pretty solid to look at anyway). We could be pretty confident of the searches as we knew the history of the ownership. So things can go quickly in Greece, with house purchase.

The stumbling block at that time was that, in the Dodecanese, there was a special layer of legislation to protect the market from those highly suspect near neighbours, the Turks. So my lawyer was going to have to pretend that I had a business on the island, the only other alternative being to have a Greek name on my contract - not a wise move as it could take huge effort and money to remove this later. So all this was set in motion, we offering the asking price of 40 million drachmas (about £80,000 then), not a lot for a 4-bedroomed 2-bathroomed antique house. Because of the timing of our finance coming through, we decided to do a 2-stage contract involving an initial deposit. Greek law dictates that if this is paid and the purchaser backs out, the deposit is lost. But if the vendor backs out, he has to pay twice the deposit. So I decided that I would pay, in mid- October, as much as I could (28 million drachmas - £56,000) for our vendor was unlikely to back out, giving me 56 million.

The rest of my father's and sons' holiday was thus spent in happy contemplation of a glorious addition to the family assets, and a fabulous holiday home for years to come. We were taking a risk, for how could we be sure the money would be there? A feeling of 'meant to be' had obviously come over us and given us the confidence to proceed.

But how did this ability to finance the place come

about? I had the money coming from my aunt's estate, but what of my father? The arrival of his money is an incredible story, famous in the press of the late 90s. He had a female relative, never married, a sort of second cousin with the same surname who had worked since 1928 in her own firm of chartered accountants in Edinburgh, ending up with offices in two adjoining properties in Charlotte Square in Edinburgh (and you don't get much of a better address than that.) She had a house in Blackhall, another in Merchiston, and a cottage at St Abb's . She had an impressive portfolio of stocks and shares. She had a telegram coming from the Queen for her 100th birthday in December 1997: but she died, one month before it. She had left no will. Her poor lawyer explained that he had acquired most of his grey hairs trying to get her to sign innumerable wills he had prepared for her over the years.

So my father, the eldest male relative in the vicinity, was made chief executor, shortly to acquire 4 co-executors, many of them elderly. A firm was engaged to trace potential claimants from round the world, for over the years emigration had split up certain branches of the family, as revealed by the family tree which also had to be produced. Sadly the first firm made a mess of it, not advertising widely enough and in the right places, so there was a delay in the whole process while someone more competent was found. Eventually, after a great deal of strain on the executors, especially my hyper-conscientious father, 800 false claimants were investigated and rejected, and 25 equal shares (stirpes, under Scottish law) decided on. Some of these would go to people outright, those of my father's generation. Others would be divided among the progeny, my generation. And the amount was considerable. The old lady ended up being worth £7.5 million. Needless to say, the taxman got his share almost immediately - about £2.3 million.

But the rest of us had a nail-biting two year wait, while houses and shares were sold (and thank goodness they were, overruling the wishes of one executor, for the stock market dived shortly afterwards). The vast amount of beautiful furniture, silver, paintings etc that she had acquired in her lifetime was either 'bought' by the family as part of their share or sent to auction at Christie's. It was strange, going round her house in Blackhall, to think that she lived in the back kitchen and one small bedroom, with no central heating, while the rest of the house was a treasure trove, featuring no less than seven grandfather clocks. So, most of us in the family have some solid memento of that incredible time and of the life of this amazing woman, Helen M. Lowe, CA, MBE.

The holiday had some other notable events, in particular the hair-raising trip to the Monastery up the narrow road on the edge of the precipices. The baker would give lifts in his truck, and my sons were in the back, with Dad and myself in the cab. All went well till shortly above the old village when our driver met someone coming the other way at a particularly difficult spot, a blind hairpin bend. He then proceeded to reverse round the corner on the edge of a lethal cliff - a heart-stopping moment indeed. The boys were fascinated with the high plateau where the Monastery sat, and the opportunity to get within stroking range of the donkeys, which Dimitris the caretaker still used for his transport to and from Emborio. The little Church of St John the Baptist was memorable for its striking and rather gruesome icons and wall paintings featuring the severed head of the Saint. It seemed that the big Festival at the end of August was dedicated to this Saint and his ghastly end.

James had made a mistake when snorkelling and stayed out too long with no protection on his back, resulting in horrendous sunburn, and the need to sleep on his front, his back smeared in yoghurt, for a few days. Luckily he had recovered fully before my 49th birthday party which was held at Nektarios's taverna of course. They excelled themselves with a delicious *mezedes* (a series of small 'starter' type dishes), while the baker's wife had produced a lovely chocolate cake.

And James wisely wore a t-shirt for his subsequent snorkelling expeditions, on our trip to Areta bay, and during the Alimnia picnic, on the deserted island, half an hour's sail away. Here there was a magnificent double bay, once used by various navies, notably the WWII Germans, as an anchorage and submarine base. There was a famous incident involving a party of British commandos who were being aided by the Greeks then inhabiting the island. Unfortunately the commandos were captured, sent up North and reputedly shot. The islanders were forced to leave their homes and settle on Kalkos. Most would never return to Alimnia.

It was poignant to wander round the village, and see the paintings of ships done by bored Italian seamen, while the German barracks round in the outer bay showed nostalgic drawings of home, be it striking sketches of pine forests, or jolly scenes from the *bierkeller.* More than anything, these mementos bring home the reality of war, and how it affects the individual caught up in it. And especially chilling for me was the thought that some of these homesick soldiers and sailors were no older, possibly younger, than my son Thomas, then

19. My boys, normally chatty and joshing, were struck into a sombre mood by these graffiti, so they may well have had the same thoughts as me.

A few days later, just before the Festival of the Virgin Mary (held on the Eve, August the 14th, in the Church) James and Thomas and I found ourselves up at the Church of the Virgin in Chorio, en route to the Castle. To our great delight, the Church was open, for a posse of local ladies was cleaning and polishing in preparation for the annual use of a church whose ancient smoke-blackened frescos were a wonder and a treasure, not to be accessed in an unsupervised manner. Most churches had a key or other latch on the outside which kept wandering animals out but allowed visitors to gain entry. But only the priest could issue the key for this special church. So we saw it, for the first and only time, in daylight, which I never have again.

Just as well we had such a peaceful and uncluttered viewing, because the place was heaving on the night of the 14th when, having stood interminably in the queue for a place in one of the open trucks used as transport up the hairpin road, we found ourselves seated at the trestle tables in the yard of the village hall. High above us up the steep path, the Church glowed golden against the blackness of the Castle lowering against a midnight blue sky.

Amazingly, a mass catering enterprise had sprung up in the hall kitchen, masterminded as usual by Litsa, the best cook on the island, and widowed mother of 3 grown up children, all working on Kalkos. This diminutive lady was an absolute powerhouse, cooking for her family from produce she grew or made from the milk of the many sheep and goats the family still kept. When she was not cleaning in the house, she would be up the hill feeding or watering her animals and chickens, or weeding the vegetable patch, making cheese or her fabled *keftedes* (meatballs). Another speciality was the (heart-stoppingly calorific) *Kalkos pasta*, a recipe where melted butter played a major role, both in caramelising the onions and in binding the mass of home made pasta shreds and cheese topping. It was when I once saw her younger son demolishing two large helpings of this (I struggling with half a portion) that I got a clue as to why all the children were of somewhat portly dimensions, though Marcos the elder son made an effort to fight against the lure of his mother's bountiful provision and succeeded in slimming down considerably, aided by his enthusiasm and talent for dancing.

But tonight's fare was laid down by tradition and funded by the Church. A mixed salad was followed by *fava,* a sort of split pea stew, and very tasty. Along with it came the specially spiced bread made in huge 50cm roundels by the baker that morning, and blessed in the Church before being hastily hacked into chunks and carried round the throng in huge baskets. After the meal, and before the dancing began, the priest went round the assembly with his attendants carrying the icon of the Virgin, which the devout wanted to kiss. Following a short speech by the priest, the *lyra* band struck up the fabulous lilting 'fiddle' music, with its elements both of Scottish jauntiness and the slinkier rhythms of gypsy playing.

Annoyingly, and sometimes dangerously, the dance floor was tiny, which meant a restriction in the numbers and the style of those joining in. Chairs were crashed into, feet trampled, and we were glad to have chosen seats some way back from the action. The effect of the incandescent celebration under the black velvet sky with the mountains glowing faintly grey all around, and sending back spine-tingling echoes of the mournful sweetness of the *lyra* . Here it was again, that feeling of awe at the smallness of human beings and their little patch of warm communion among all this raw insouciant nature.

The atmosphere the next night was quite different, for then the village of Emborio was taken over by crowded tables full of reunited Greeks, with the visiting British, Italians and German yachtsmen struggling to find a table for dinner. Needless to say, tables at the restaurants nearest the open village square were at a premium. I was so glad my sons had experienced this Festival, and its amazing atmosphere, (leaving aside the embarrassment of watching their mother dancing). They were never to come at this time again, and it was a perfect end to what had been an extraordinary holiday in our family's history. The sight of so many Greeks villagers and visitors, and the occasional intrepid foreigner (including myself occasionally) proceeding in a huge ring or even two rings one inside the other, round the large square, arms on shoulders, brought a lump to the throat. Especially affecting was to watch the children at the end of the line, fumbling and stumbling, but gamely trying to pick up, and being indulged by their elders.

Indeed it was at this time that the general attitude to children became especially noticeable. I had often been a little surprised to see young children staying up late at night, running around playing with their peers once they had dined with their parents, who had now proceeded to a bar or lingered in the taverna. Still thinking in British terms, I felt the need for some babysitting to be going on, so that the adults could relax in peace. But when I think back from now, how sterile and strange it would have been. The British families, of which there were not many in those days, found that their children instantly tapped into this free-ranging society and would be running around with new friends with whom they shared not a whit of communication except the universal energy of youth.

CHAPTER 19 - ART AND THE HEART

I am a gregarious soul, much fond of witty conversation, so although I enjoyed my more solitary activities of star-gazing and moon-watching I was always keen for company among the ex-pats and often the visitors too. One chap who soon made himself known was David, a school teacher, who used to come for about a month at a time in the school holidays, and had indeed been doing that for 11 years by then. David was a reasonably attractive guy, tall, with nice features, and a great sense of fun. The only drawback was that he spent his entire time in an alcoholic haze, his first beer of the day being about 10 a.m., to be followed by a continuous consumption, topped up with retsina and later Metaxa in the evening.

David's inebriated state obviously made him feel a great sense of bonhomie towards everyone, and he was inclined to stop off and chat continually, as one was trying to progress along the harbour-front, making a planned time of arrival at any destination very difficult. I often wondered if I should be sponsored by the visitors to go out with him more often, as his even more annoying trait was to attach himself to people at their table and join them, even if they just wanted a quiet dinner by themselves. I have a photograph of myself in that year, in Petro's taverna, sitting on David's knee unwilling having just been grabbed from behind. He is grinning, but my face is quite a study. David got to know my father and sons of course, and they still ask after him, for under all the difficult behaviour the man had a good kind heart. He had suffered much stress after the death of his father, and this had affected his ability to cope in the primary school where he worked. Immediately, given my history of emotional trauma in teaching, I felt a kinship.

David rescued me rather neatly from a lonely plight the night I unwisely decided to attend the party down at the cantina, and found myself alone, unable to communicate, among a bunch of young Greeks. David came along in the baker's truck, for they were great pals. That was another annoying trait though, this boasting on David's part about being one of the in crowd and how much he could get them to do for him. The baker was and is a great practical joker, and David always played up to it, though somehow he always ended up the object of the Greeks amusement rather than an equal partner in it. Of course it crossed my mind that Martin might be worth cultivating, as that rare commodity, a single man. But somehow his rather buffoonish image combined with the continual drunken haze rendered him totally lacking in any sexual attraction, which for me is more important than most people would expect at my age.

I had a brief fling with one of the teachers but found him disappointing, probably because no one could really hold a candle to the frustrating attractions of Nektarios. It was the beginning of the end for my affection towards him when I discovered that he had lost a little painting of the Monastery which I had shown him and he had admired. To give someone a present of something precious to oneself and have it treated in a feckless and uncaring manner was hurtful. I cringe now when I think of the stupid way I threw myself at him, and let him use me, but then I have always been a bit of a dope in my relations with men.

I was a bit taken aback when it was revealed that there was a plan to arrange a marriage between Nektarios and a local girl, a buxom long-haired beauty, younger daughter of one of the boatmen. She was sent to work in the taverna alongside him, presumably for them to get to know each other, but she seemed less than enthusiastic about this idea, and about him. That the marriage did not come off is a mercy for her, for it turned out that Nektarios was ultimately of the gay persuasion, and not keen on staying on Kalkos, but rather drawn to North Africa, which would have left her both devoid of a proper husband and a long way from the support of her family.

In the end, just before I left Kalkos, some wine having been consumed, I made a tape, in French, which blathered on some hopeless romantic drivel as a sort of 'closure' with Nektarios. To my horror, I forgot about this tape when returning the machine to the office, and had to hastily contact Maggie for her to rescue it from public consumption. She did listen to it and asked me just how drunk I had been. I explained that, while I had sampled a glass or two, it was the difficulty of speaking in French throughout which had produced a voice so deep and slow and slurry.

If I had wasted some artwork on Nektarios, it was not wasted on everyone, for my painted plates were quite a hit, even though my watercolours were wince-makingly bad at that time (my chalk drawings somewhat better.) I had some wonderful felt-tip type crayons which produced bright colours and were easy to handle, although not as durable as I would have liked despite the oven firing. I also, with a certain mess and smell, produced painted glassware, an initiative I had begun in the UK, where one could buy pretend leading and transparent spirit based colours. I decorated Harvey's Bristol Cream bottles, that wonderful blue, with silver 'leading'. I painted sun-catchers, circular pieces of Perspex, pierced with a hole for a hanging string. And I can proudly boast of my first ever commission, a zodiac sun-catcher for Leo, requested by Manolis from the bar where I held my first exhibition that September. Karen invested in the first of her still-growing collection of my 'octopus' plates. I remember taking photos of all my plates, on the stones of the path outside my little house, and still kept in a little album.

These stones saw me doing my exercises in the morning, mainly skipping on the spot and a bit of stretching, much to the bemusement of the local Greeks. But it was on a night in August that I took my most unusual exercise out there. Night after night, I had lain in the baking heat, listening to the often strong hot wind blowing the dust around on the tiles. This was my first Greek Summer and I was struggling with the relentless heat, the lack of variety in the weather (oh no not another cloudless hot sunny day!) and the maddening 'hair-dryer' quality of the wind. So this night, once again I heard the pattering of the dust, so I thought, but then it seemed a little different. I got up, at nearly 5.a.m. and looked out. Rain! Lots of it! Without hesitation or shoes, I rushed out and danced on the path in my nightshirt, delirious with the refreshment, the relief. Once back in the house I felt a bit foolish, but resigned to the fact that everyone regarded me as their friendly local eccentric anyway. But amusingly, talking in the bars, I later discovered a secret sisterhood (Jenny among them) of ex-pat rain-dancers.

As for the village dancers, the greatest Festival was to come at the end of August, the Festival of St John - commemorating the beheading of John the Baptist. The religious festivities and subsequent dancing took place up at the Monastery of St John on the high plateau almost at the Western end of the island. Some years before finishing about 1995, a road had been built, single track, to assist the villagers with access to the Monastery and the mountain churches. This was a modern endowment from the residents of Tarpon Springs in Florida, where many Kalkos Greeks had settled when invited to go over to service the infant sponge fishing industry in the Gulf of Mexico. Transport of all sorts was added to hired minibuses to carry the many visitors, most of them Greeks returning from all over the World to their families' ancestral home. Some would stay the night in special buildings, gifted to the Monastery by their family, or on camp beds in the cells or out on the terraces.

I went up with Sally, Phil not being at all interested in the whole business. We sat up on a terrace, with the 'cells' at our backs, observing the scene below. The courtyard was brilliantly lit with lights hanging from the ancient central cypress tree. The priest conducted the service, the icon was carried around for the faithful to kiss, and the bread was blessed. But something was happening in the cell behind us which caught our attention and distracted us from the religious ceremony below. Indeed, women of the world though we were, Sally and I were rather shocked to realise what was going on at the same time as the priest was uttering his blessings. But there could be no mistaking the fact that there were 2 girls in that cell inviting a succession of young men into the room, it would appear for oral sex, underlined when one of the girls emerged briefly, ostentatiously wiping her mouth, while her latest customer wandered off, unselfconsciously adjusting his private parts in his trousers. It seemed that the Monastery warden's daughters had been used by their father from an early age, and therefore thought nothing of helping ease the sexual tension in these young men, however inappropriate the timing. Could we just say it left a bad taste in the mouth?

The ceremony over, the tables set out all around, were used to serve out a delicious lamb, accompanied by the blessed bread, now chopped up. It was a wonder that this could be achieved in such a setting, with everything having to be transported up the mountain. Indeed, visits to the Monastery in the 2 weeks preceding the Festival could be difficult at the warden and his wife would already be getting stressed with all the preparations, including the special visits of the water tanker, for they were not on the mains, but reliant on their huge sterna, which would be under great pressure.

Once the meal was over, it was time for the music and dancing, with 'guest' appearances by local *lyra* players and singers, adding to the texture of the occasion, which was generally favoured by the appearance of Ilias, a great player and singer from Karpathos (and quite a dish to boot!) The great rings of dancers wound around the cypress tree in slow and stately communion, then faster more intricate dances mingled in. I had by this time mastered one dance, and I went down to join in. But after that I was happy to go home. Sally and I both had work the next day, and we also realised with some dismay that we had omitted to secure ourselves a lift down the mountain, and were going to have to walk all the way, which could take nearly 2 hours even in the light and more serviceable shoes.

We had not gone very far when we were overtaken by Anargiros the travelling vegetable salesman in his pick up truck. He stopped and offered us a lift, Sally in the middle of the front seat, and I (luckily for me!) by the other door. About a kilometre down the mountain, we passed a group of visitors walking down, and I was surprised that Anargiros did not offer them a lift too. (How naïve of me!) The conversation was necessarily limited, but apparently Anargiros was quite active in other departments, giving Sally's (rather shapely) thighs a good fondling. As soon as we got to the first crossroads in the town, Sally insisted we got out there. When she told me what had happened, we realised that our kind chauffeur had thought he had bought himself 2 women for the night.

No such hazards attended the dancing in the village the following night, where again the lights were strung, and the tavernas full to bursting (especially those nearest the town square.) One might as well be there and join in, for it was clear that there would be little sleep for anyone. Indeed, a common practice was to dance the night away then get on the 06.00 boat to leave in the morning. The great Ilias and his band once again played and sang, with hardly a break, and the village united in the great concentric rings, arms on shoulders. Interspersed were the energetic performances of the *sousta* and other fast intricate dances which I longed to learn. But rather as Maggie found she could not turn her facility for picking up languages by ear to learning Greek, so I found it impossible to suss out the syncopated movements of the footwork by observation.

After the Festival, suddenly the island seemed deserted, for the huge influx of Greeks had gone, and the Italian season had ended. The Northern children were about to go back to school, the Greeks a little later (and UK people think our teachers have long holidays!) The next highlight was the ELIAMEP conference, a mainstay of the Hotel, where fledgling diplomats from Eastern European countries came to practice their negotiating skills. Most people could see, however, that it was just an excuse for a giant 'beano' in a fabulously beautiful place. The Hotel itself, presided over by the redoubtable Mr Michalis, who had taken the lease, was a rather old dinosaur, with 70s décor and fittings, though beloved of its regular clientele for its faded charm and reasonable prices.

The Hotel had been developed, at about the same time as our wonderful new house had been restored, to accommodate young Greeks staying together on the newly designated 'Island of Peace and Friendship'. These restorations for this purpose were a UNESCO initiative, though their conference lapsed, to be replaced by ELIAMEP, and occasionally a doctor's conference. The Hotel could also be used for functions, birthday parties, weddings, concerts, all of which I attended in that first year. The 2 room blocks were attached to the central function hall, which had been converted out of the old sponge drying warehouse. One could look up and see the angled rafters from which the sponges were hung, the breeze allowed to blow through to speed the drying.

I also discovered that amazing and unlikely-sounding dish lobster in red sauce with spaghetti, which was Michali's speciality and an outstanding delicacy. That there was an Italian influence there was undoubted, and indeed the Hotel was immensely popular with the visiting Italians who formed the bulk of its non-Conference customers. My erstwhile companion David the teacher had been coming to Kalkos for many years and always stayed in the Hotel, where he could get as long a stay as he wanted, unlike with the companies who usually wanted 1 or 2 week bookings only.

A very arresting feature of the Hotel's main room was the collection of striking paintings interspersed around, some of Kalkos houses, some of boating scenes or beach adventures, but one in particular, unforgettable, a portrait of a fisherman, swarthy, muscled, staring with wild eyes out of the canvas. There must have been some connection between one of the artists and the family of Michalis and Manolis, for I noticed paintings in a similar style adorning Manoli's bar at the other end of the harbour. I was quite good at portraits, having won a First Prize at the County Show some years before for a painting in acrylic of my old heart-throb John Sessions. I resolved to have another go, and began with a pencil study of Sally, of which I was very proud and she very pleased when I gave it to her. I hatched an idea to paint some of the locals, and indeed took photos of them for such a purpose, but then got put off by the story of Joan the shopkeeper. When she used photos of local people in her calendar there was a big outcry. Of course she did not tell me at the time that she had omitted to ask the people's permission to use their photos for this purpose. But still, my art idea went into abeyance, for the end of my season was beckoning and I had preparations to make.

CHAPTER 20 - SETTLING INTO NAPLOS

'A pretty neat town' was Sofia's assessment of this small city by the sea. On my first visit, I had to agree. Edinburgh-born, I needed to be near the sea, and Naplos has a magnificent sea front lined with public gardens at one end, and apartment buildings with cafes and tavernas below for more than a kilometre at the other. For the people on the nearby islands, it was the metropolis. For the cruise ships, it is the best port for Meteora, one of the wonders of the world, with monasteries perched on incredible towers of rock.

For me, at first, it was a shopping centre I could cope with without getting lost, being set on a grid of streets running straight up from and parallel to the sea. Early in my stay on Stargos, I had needed a suitcase, my previous one having expired under the strain of hauling my winter clothes – and my cruise clothes – to Greece. My boss, Sofia, had been intimidated by the thought of my turning up in glamorous sparkly frocks, but mostly it was my big climbing boots and duffle coat in the rainy Stargos Winter. But the sparkly frocks had had to come with me, and cluttered up the wardrobe excitingly, whispering of a treat to come which I could not afford.

I met Sofia's American friend Glenda for dinner, seeing Naplos at night this time, with the lights of the mountain villages star-studding the slopes behind the city. This was the beginning of my future there, making contacts, making a relationship with the place. So, as I came towards the end of the school year in Stargos, I was fixed up with interviews at some of the many frontistirios, and made my choice, of a school where Glenda liked the boss, Lina. But I knew from what Lina and I discussed that I would be working at another school to get enough hours. I was to find a more challenging situation when I finally did arrive.

But Yianni the poseur, suave in his suede jacket and misplaced testosterone pride was worth meeting if only for the amusement of watching how dumbfounded he was when I turned him down. I had heard of the slavery at that school. At another, the two women who worked together seemed very intense but not to be altogether seeing eye to eye, so I could imagine being an uncomfortable sounding board in the middle, not being able to do right for doing in wrong in the eyes of one or the other.

Mindful of the possessions (at least now devoid of sparkly frocks) which were stored in Stargos, too much to carry in one go, I arranged with Lina to post stuff to her school (having discovered that Greek internal post, although not the fastest, was at least amazingly reasonable in price). So I collected some cardboard boxes and over my last couple of weeks on Kalkos set about sending off books, winter clothes etc. My last contacts with my reluctant amour Nektarios were when I borrowed his 'sack trolley' to move my parcels to the Post Office.

Meanwhile, I had been preparing information regarding my set up in the office and procedure with clients, in order for Sarah's husband Sam, and later Sarah herself to take over for the last weeks of the season, as agreed what seemed so long ago, back in May. It was then that it really came home to me how much I had put into the job, which had always had that 'make it up as you go along' sort of remit.

In mid-September, I wrenched myself away from my new friends and the lovely place I had found, and got on the plane to Athens and the bus to Naplos. At least by now I was aware of what I was facing at the dreadful Athens bus station. The one thing which had improved for me since my first arrival in Greece, and indeed since I had fixed up my job in Naplos was that my finances had taken a turn for the better because I had received payment from my aunt's estate. This put me in a different position psychologically, since I did not actually need the job to survive, and I had the happy prospect of at least being able to pay the deposit for my wonderful house on Kalkos.

All went pretty well at first, when I arrived at Lina's school, though I sensed she had been none too happy to accommodate my parcels. Strange that, considering that, firstly, the building was huge with many spare rooms and secondly, that the term had not started yet. She took me to the temporary accommodation she had fixed for me, rather a nice boarding house (though without breakfast) almost on the seafront. It was a long way from the school however, so I soon got used to timing my walks, it taking at least 35 minutes to get up the hill to her establishment. I was coming in to study the books I was to use and discuss which classes I would take and when. Lina also fixed me up with an email address, which was to prove a lifeline once I discovered the expensive but invaluable internet café in the back streets of the town centre.

After a couple of days, Lina dropped what was a bit of a bombshell. I was to be taken to meet the other school bosses for whom I would be working. And there were 5 of them (2 of them partners in one school). So, 5 schools in all, not what I was expecting of course. I was charming at the meeting, if a little shell-shocked. Now I knew I had agreed that more than one school was needed but I felt like a subject of the 'white slave' trade with all these women wanting a piece of me. And the trouble was that the economic argument was right. I needed the hours to make any sort of living, and even then it was pitiful.

But it got worse. It turned out that, unlike Sofia, who had been determined to do the right thing, none of these women was prepared to pay the IKA National Insurance contributions for me, so they were forcing me to become self-employed, there being some loophole whereby if I only did so many hours they could claim I was just bought in and was not an employee. Lina was the one who employed me most, and probably was over this total, but I was dragged into the scam, like it or not. My pride and feistiness, let alone my honesty, rebelled against all this, but I was not prepared to admit I had been taken in, and that I might find the whole thing a bit much. The irony of the economic argument was that although they claimed to be giving me these hours to help me get more money, making me pay self-employed TEBE was much more expensive for me and mitigated against any advantage. All they had to pay was a little bit of tax.

I had to get an accountant, receipt books, translations of papers from the UK, lots of Greek papers with lots of colourful stamps, and pay about £90 a month insurance. It would have paid me better not to work at all. And all on the paltry 2200 drachmas an hour they were paying – and paying for the hours I worked in the school of course, not the preparation and marking time at home. It's a mug's game in other words, and the only reason I put up with these sharks for any time was that I still had the idea of getting enough frontline experience to make a move to teacher education in TEFL, as my friend Margaret, who had done TEFL straight from University, had achieved.

This would have been bad enough, but when we started to look for somewhere for me to live, things took a truly bizarre turn. Here were these women, all wanting the advantage of having an intelligent native speaker to work with their students, but they were simply not prepared to pay for this person to be accommodated properly so that she would be happy and well-adjusted to her work. I was taken, by Athina, one of the more motherly of the school bosses, to see what I can only describe as a hovel. One room in a semi-basement, none too clean, it had no furniture, and a barely adequate bathroom. All it had going for it was the largish outside space, but as we were heading for Winter, this seemed no attraction. I was horrified that they would even consider putting me there, but this was the level they were prepared to pay for. My heart hardened another layer.

But what I did was offer to pay the extra for a better standard of place. So Lina and I started looking, and on about the 4th try found just the place, a large empty flat very close to 2 of the schools, in a nice area. It had a petrol heater, which was a bit scary, but I guessed I would learn to cope. Athina lent me a sofa, strangely called a *kanape* in Greek, a word usually associated with a small tasty snack at a cocktail party. Maybe they are called that because you sit on sofas while eating them?

Since I was now going to be based quite a long way from 3 of the schools, I needed some transport, so as not to waste an inordinate amount of time walking, not an attractive prospect with heavy books to carry anyway. I presented myself at a bicycle shop on one of the main streets and was delighted to discover just what I was looking for. It was quite heavy and solid, a real workhorse of a general road bike, with fat tyres and simple gears on a low bar 'lady's' frame, and a strong carrying grid with straps over the rear mudguard. 70,000 drachmas (about £140) were well-spent on my new 'runabout'. I was a bit over-protective of it at first, although I had purchased a lock, and I would pull it up into the stairwell of my apartment overnight. This can't have been popular with the landlord, for the tyres made black marks on the walls. I spent a couple of days practising the journeys to and from the schools, and trying out routes between them. Luckily, Naplos's grid system of streets was easy to follow, with all but the widest on an alternate one-way system. I soon began to get fit, as the place sloped up the foothills of the mountains behind, gently at first, but more sharply at the back of the town, where Tharani's school was. Round the bay where I lived it was flat, so my route to Mina and Athina's schools, only 5 and 10 minutes away, was easy, as was the journey to the shops, down in the flat part of town near the sea.

Once I had settled on the flat, I had to get a bed and

various other items of furniture as I needed storage for my books and general paraphernalia. It was quite handy to be only on the bike because it was then easy to persuade the firms to deliver various items (at a price). The most important was the bed, as I could not stand too many more nights on the sofa. After that, I found 2 cane units and a rather clever folding round table, from the same shop. Flights of fancy took over more (of course with an eye on what would suit the house in Kalkos) when I found the 'Eastern' furniture shop, which had 2 rather attractive wrought iron and leather chairs, and a gorgeous mirror with a carved wooden surround.

Lina had helped me get a second-hand table top cooker and fridge, though it had to be said the former was far from attractive, as the seller had reneged on her promise to clean it up before we got it delivered and I had to scrape away years of grease from the interior and shelves. It was a big kitchen, with cupboards on floor and wall along one wall, with the petrol heater, the only source of heating in the apartment on the other wall, which had the doors to the bedroom and bathroom to either side of it. The other wall was the door to the living room, the opposite wall having a suitable space for my tall shelf unit where I kept the course books for my multifarious classes.

Settling into the house was easy compared to the paperwork parts of getting registered. Admittedly, the hospital visit, though bewildering for a non-Greek speaker, was mercifully quite quick, though I was a bit taken aback to find that the blood test they had done was to find out if I was clear of syphilis. When it came to the chest x-ray, which at least I did manage to have taken this time, I had to smirk grimly at the fact that the doctor I presented myself to for the okay did not appear even to look at the film properly. That I had it in my possession seemed to be enough. Well at least that was the first stage over.

Now I had to tackle the police station to get my residency papers. Here we met a stumbling block because one of the documents they needed to see was away at the Embassy in Athens being examined, and the Police would not accept a photocopy. Here I turned in faithfully about twice a week, having realised that persistence might well be rewarded. Finally the charming young lieutenant got so fed up of seeing my eager countenance across his desk that he capitulated and agreed to photocopy my photocopy and pretend he had seen the original.

I now acquired various mysterious registration books at TEBE the self-employed National Insurance Office, some of which were for making payments, and others for medical claims for treatment, drugs, etc. I was introduced to Yiorgos, Athina's lovely English-speaking accountant, who was to be a great support to me over the coming months, shepherding me through the registration of my business and acquisition of a tax number.

So there I was, legal, signed up in all sorts of official ways. But I needed communication. For those I could not contact by email through the internet cafe, I had to find another system, and discovered the fax sending service at the Post Office. Here I could send letters to Sarah in Stargos, and Maggie, Phil and Sally in Kalkos. I had purchased rather a nice mobile phone in Kalkos, but my boss, visiting, had 'borrowed' it and not returned it, so I was in need of another, essential for keeping in touch with the schools, and my family, till I managed to get a land line installed. I was impressed to find that OTE the Greek phone company were pretty efficient and clued-up, the first of the Greek public companies to get their act together. I found the process of ordering a landline simple and quick, but while I was waiting for my turn I was amused to see a big Greek guy in the same section talking on his mobile. This man was about 6 foot 3 and built like a wrestler, with a tree-trunk neck and hands like bunches of bananas. However, to his enormous ear he held daintily between his thumb and forefinger a tiny mobile phone. Goodness me, I thought, the only time a Greek man would ever boast of having something smaller than anyone else!

I needed entertainment too, and though I knew that watching Greek TV would be good for me, it was too much like hard work, and hardly inspiring given the strange character of most programmes. They seemed to consist mainly of ridiculous comedies presented in the full 'coarse acting' style of an amateur pantomime, or interminable current affairs programmes where lots of talking heads all argued with each other at once, in a cacophony which would do nothing for my understanding of Greek. So I targeted a little TV/video combined set I found in an electrical shop at the end of the harbour, which was duly delivered, and which I proceeded to employ when I returned after the teaching evening, either to watch the English-speaking film at 9 pm, or a video I had borrowed from one of the 2 video rental libraries I patronised. At one of them, I had a rather funny experience, when I went in looking for a certain film which had been well-reviewed in the UK, starring Gwynneth Paltrow and John Hannah.

However when I asked the assistant (who knew me quite well by then),

'Do you have 'Sliding Doors'?'

I was surprised and amused to find him rushing over to the shop door and demonstrating that, no, the doors opened inward on their hinges.

Sitting in front of my film, I would have a snack of crackers and *tzaziki* (yoghurt and cucumber dip, spiced) or *hummus* with a bit of salad. Although I was able to have a cooked lunch during the day, before my teaching hours began, I could never be bothered to cook late in the evening, not a good time to eat a big meal anyway. The delights of solo eating out were not many, after all, though I did try out a couple of the local tavernas. As long as I had my supply of red wine, I was happy with minimal (and of course cheaper) standards of home catering, often based on pulses, lentil bolognese and lentil soup being my usual staples. If only I could have conquered the smoking, I would have been pursuing a rather healthy lifestyle.

I came in for a bit of criticism from Lina over the smoking. Although a smoker herself, she was one of those lucky souls who can last for hours and hours then really enjoy a few fags. I however am a raving addict when I am doing it, unable to last half an hour without the craving. Thus, I would be found rushing out of the building in the short breaks between classes, to have a quick puff round the corner, in the vain hope of being unseen by the kids while doing so.

'You are a chain smoker!' announced Lina, rather unfairly, for chain smoking is literally lighting one from another, which I was certainly not doing at my rate of one an hour.

Certainly some of my classes really tested my nerves and I would have been a wreck without my regular injection of nicotine. The younger ones would be unable to do the work, the older ones unwilling to do it. The children at Lina's school, where I would do 4 hours end to end, ranged in age from about 9 up to the Michigan and Cambridge classes at about 16 and 17. The girls in the senior class I found a bit resistant to my pushing them on their interpretation and composition exercises. I wondered if they had got a bit of an inflated idea of their competence or maybe I was being too fussy.

There was one lad, however, about whom I worried, for his parents were pushing him far too hard. He should have gone for the Michigan, for he was just about capable of passing that. However, family pride dictated otherwise, and he was being pushed in for the Cambridge, far beyond his abilities. It broke my heart to watch him struggle and damage his self-esteem in the process. I wanted to appeal to the parents of this poor lad, who was also doing high level courses in French and Maths on top of his normal school work. I told Lina my concern, with which she agreed, but said the parents were adamant. I tried to think of ways to help him, for he had not the more sophisticated grasp of the actual day to day use of English which the Cambridge demands, let alone the detailed knowledge of grammar which must be demonstrated. I got various video recordings made of a range of programmes in the UK - current affairs, football commentary, nature documentary - so that he could immerse himself in how English was used in these contexts. I gave them to him, but I'm not sure he ever bothered to look at them.

In the other schools, I generally only had one class to

worry about, usually the older ones. I had the Michigan class at Tharani's. up the hill, my favourite session of the week, with some excellent students in it. At Theodosia and Eleni's, I had a similar level, quite a big class and thus harder to control. Mina gave me First Certificate level, with rather a good book to work from. It was at Athina's that I met my best student, with whom I did individual classes towards the Cambridge, as well as doing the small group Michigan class with 5 in it.

Although I had 5 schools to worry about, I never had more than 2 of them in one day, and was free after midday on a Saturday. Mind you, especially with Lina's classes, I found myself pounding on the keyboard of my word processor to produce extra enrichment exercises to practice points of grammar, thus putting in many hours over and above normal preparation and marking time. But to be truthful I rather enjoyed the exercise.

So my teaching routine was established, my transport and communication in place. Now the community, and the local area, were waiting for me to explore.

CHAPTER 21 - AUTUMN MEETINGS

A familiar lifeline amongst the strangeness of adjusting to a new place and many new people was my friendship with Sarah, still working on Stargos and its sister islands, only a hydrofoil ride away from Naplos. We decided that I would snatch a short break, but I had to go to Skipos, the second island, where Sarah was based for a few days. I duly booked the hydrofoil and arrived in time to spend the afternoon at her favourite beach. Here, unlike on Kalkos, one could sit and watch the sun go down, which I found quite entrancing. But before that I had been treated to the awe-inspiring sight of Sarah (ever-sporty) zooming up and down on water skis.

We were sharing a little apartment, which had twin beds. Nevertheless, Sarah was over-anxious, I felt, that the landlady might get the impression that we were lesbian lovers. Well, I thought, if you were that worried you should have booked us separate rooms, surely. I impressed Sarah at dinner by managing to ask for the bill in Greek. And from the people at the table behind I learned a new word 'apopse' meaning 'tonight'. At that time I thought it was amazing that Sarah's Greek was so poor considering how long she had been working out there. I was later to realise that it depended on the one hand on your natural aptitude (and complex about making a fool of yourself) and on the other whom it was that you typically worked with.

I had a great time, but I was to get a major shock in the morning when I went to get the hydrofoil which I had to be on in order to get to work later. The thing was full. Sarah had assured me all would be ok, but here there was a large party of Dutch tourists en route to the airport. I was so stressed that I got rather upset in the ticket office, and was faced with an uncooperative and unsympathetic girl behind the desk. She announced,

'I don't like you so I'm not going to help you!'

This was outrageous. I was beside myself, but evidently further appeals to her would only make matters worse. Saints be praised, her boss came into the agency just in time, and I appealed to him, whereupon, cleverly circumventing the spleen of his employee, he beckoned me outside. His tip was to go and beg help from the captain of the hydrofoil, whom I could see through the open window.

Well desperate times call for desperate actions, and I proceeded to fall to my knees theatrically opposite the window (I think I even wrung my hands together) and explained my plight, begging to be helped. This bit of Greek drama as performed by a Scotswoman did the trick and I found myself being allowed aboard. This was possible with these hydrofoils in those days as people could sit or stand outside, so the number of seats inside could be quietly exceeded. I managed to look suitably grateful while my tight-lipped former nemesis resentfully bashed the keys to issue my ticket. I even blurted out a thank you.

I needed no encouragement to stand outside on the hydrofoil, for I loved it as a 'fairground ride', with the excitement of watching the foaming churning tail zooming out behind, so close below one's position. And so I was back in Naplos, with no option but to apply the nose to the grindstone. But I had spotted someone on the hydrofoil in whom I took what seems now to be a bizarre interest, Alexandros, one of the seamen working aboard. I think I fancied him because of a certain resemblance to John Sessions the actor, for whom I had long cherished an unrequited passion (never likely to be requited, given his gayness). On closer inspection, Alexandros proved to have rather dodgy teeth, something I am usually particular about (though, curiously, my ex-husband Peter had dodgy teeth too). But there was a definite attraction. I managed to acquire his phone number. However, despite a couple of attempts we never managed to fix a meeting. Perhaps Alexandros was fazed by having a woman pursuing him rather than the reverse.

Barely 4 weeks after my early departure from Kalkos, and still within the long season, I found myself set to return. The first contract for the house was due, and I managed to get a bit of weekend leave to make the trip to Rhodes, with always in my mind the chance to nip over to Kalkos. It was a late morning meeting, so my hopes for the trip rose. But they began to fray at the edges as people rolled in late, and the reading and translating and continual signing went on and on. I only hoped that the huge cheque prepared by my bank had no mistakes on it. The lady selling the house had an enormous double barrelled Greek name which was too long for the 'field' box on the payment slip. I knew I needed about an hour in a taxi to get to the 2.30 boat. Just about 1,15pm, we were finishing, and, to my delight, the vendor said that with my large deposit paid the house was effectively mine and I could have the keys. Marvellous, I thought, but my face fell as the company revealed that no one had thought to bring a set of keys

'We need to go to my house Frances,' urged Archimedes my translator. (My father could never get over these wonderful old names still being in current use.)

'How far is that? Will I make it to the boat?' I cried, a bit exasperated.

'We'll get you a taxi,' he reassured as we sped off in his car.

At least he was quick emerging from the house, but then, with no taxi rank nearby, we were at the mercy of whatever taxi chanced by, and we were now inside the precious hour required. Archimedes spotted a taxi, a truly venerable large grey Mercedes, but, as he later confessed, his heart sank as he contemplated the character of the driver. This was a tiny gnarled individual of ancient vintage, almost lost behind the wheel of his large vehicle. While he understood where he had to go, he evidently had no concept of the need for speed. Now, I was unaccustomed to having to tell Greek taxi drivers to go faster. Indeed I did not then know the word for fast *(grigora)* but only for slowly *(siga siga)*. My lack of Greek was frustrating. In vain I bounced up and down on the seat and shouted that the boat went at 2.30. This met with zero response. We proceeded at a stately 40kph the whole way, my blood pressure hitting danger level. Fast driving skills eluded him, but my chauffeur managed to cram no less than 6 cigarettes into this journey.

But I need not have worried, for the noble Archimedes, overcome with dread at having sent me off in this unpromising transport, had phoned the boat and asked them to wait for me. So as we rumbled down the landing stage, it was like a re-run of my arrival in May, when Kostas had held the boat. And once again, to my surprise and delight, the whole boat, crew included, burst into applause as I shot out of the taxi, tossing drachmas in my wake, and scrambled aboard. This habit of applauding turns up in other circumstances too, as when a planeload of Greeks starts clapping when the pilot makes a successful landing. That always gives me the impression that there was something either chancy or voluntary about the pilot doing that.

I had nothing with me but spare knickers and a toothbrush in my handbag, but my heart was bursting with joy and relief. Better still, I discovered that the vendor's husband, whom I will call Mr K, had decided to come over to show me details of the house. Coming into Kalkos in mid-October, I was immediately struck with the changed quality of the light. There was a glorious mellow golden calm over the whole place, a different feel even from mid-September when I had left. And I had reckoned without the change in me. 4 weeks of cycling had reduced my chubbiness by nearly a stone, and I was stunning my colleagues with my slim-line glamour. I was provoking 'double-takes' all over the place.

When I got to the house, I found Mr K there ready to show me details like hot water switches, pumps etc, and to introduce me to someone who was still finishing work on the house. I had seen this fellow in the distance, as a worker at one of the tavernas, manning the grill as he did, as well as his 'day job' as a builder. Indeed, I had spotted the fact that he normally looked pretty grim and miserable. This lugubriousness seemed to be caused by his shrewish wife and noisy children. But I paid him little heed except to remark one day, while talking to David the teacher,

'Ooh, Marios smiled!'

(Marios noticed I had said this) and then

'Ooh he did it again!' (no doubt in response to my remark)

I had of course been obsessed with Nektarios as my 'love interest,' and anyway was not inclined to consider anyone who was married. But it had to be said that, now I was confronted with Marios close to and full frontal, I was stunned by how beautiful he was, with glorious curly hair, black turning silver, over a heart-shaped face enlivened by the largest, most luminous brown eyes I had ever seen. Mr K was expostulating on Mario's skill as a builder (for indeed 'twas he who had been working in there when I had seen activity through the window months ago). I was encouraged to get the said man to work on the house, as he knew it. I made a large mental note in day-glow capitals that I would indeed attempt to get this gorgeous creature working for me. (I did not at this time know his reputation for unreliability in the work department, but I admit it was his own aesthetic qualities which were uppermost in my mind).

But just as charming was Mario's shy demeanour. He did not look me in the eye for long, nor did he posture or wink, or do any of these presumptuous flirtatious bits of body language, but cast his gaze down, silently waiting to be released by Mr K from being the focus of attention. I was already smitten. I never did get the outside wall lamps Mr K had been talking about, and had asked me if I wanted installed. I still wonder which house Marios put them on.

This little interlude, on top of my recent encounter with Alexandros the hydrofoil man in Naplos, brought home to me that I definitely have a weakness for short men with curly hair, largish noses and big brown eyes. Now this is totally different from both my father and my ex-husband (tall with moderate noses and blue eyes). So it is either a reaction away from those parental or otherwise controlling men, towards the opposite; or possibly (a more colourful theory) an erotic fixation with hobbits; maybe a bit of both.

I was very excited to see everyone again, and to be sleeping in my wonderful new house. It was useful to be able to assess what sort of extra equipment we would need, and what decorative items would suit the place. But after only 2 nights in the place I had to leave to be whisked back North to my new jobs. Now the tension began, for I had committed my father and myself to buy this house, and if his money did not come through in time, we were in big trouble. The lawyer we had engaged, a highly competent but rather elusive character, was armed with my various phone numbers, and vowed to keep in touch regularly.

So I just had to wait, throwing myself into the job to keep myself from worrying. And it was helpful that Glenda, Sofia's American friend had brought me along to the Foreign Association, the Naplos version of the Stargos 'WI'. Here there were a number of women of a similar age to myself, who had been in Naplos for many years, having married a local Greek. Of course I was awestruck by their ability to speak Greek, but I was assured that it was an essential skill for a foreign wife to acquire quickly, in order to defend herself against her mother-in-law. Clearly these terrifying dragons would have kept the late Bernard Manning in misogynist jokes for years. Well of course, as that joke said, these mothers were the adored virgins of the Greek men's lives, while the men were to the mothers gods. So the poor wives had little chance of gaining any importance.

I refrained from asking how things went for the women who worked in their husbands' businesses (advised against in 'Greek Men') but I could not help myself on another topic. Bracing myself to be laughed at for my naivety, I asked one of the women how she came to get married to Yiorgos the waiter when they could not even talk to each other. Pausing, and, amazingly, not laughing, she explained,

'Well the sex was fantastic!'

Hmm, I thought, do I really believe that is enough for a relationship to last? I was a bit envious, if truth be told, for my relationship with Peter had been much more personal in basis, not born of an overwhelming passion, something I had missed out on in life, he having been my first partner. I had to remind myself that what I was seeing were the survivors of what must have been many failed pairings of Greek men and foreign girls over the years.

Funnily enough, I was shortly to be introduced to Richard, a young Englishman teaching in the city who was desperate for someone British, to talk to and go out with (on a platonic basis). Richard was of an age to be my son, though I had no objection to anyone thinking he was my 'toy-boy'. We met for the first time in a fast food restaurant, 'Goody's', (rather good actually) on the seafront. Richard told me he had come some weeks previously to tutor classes of young Greeks heading for University in the UK in Maths and Science. Here had had found the background of his students in an extremely didactic education system a terrible drawback. These kids, he said, were so used to parrot-fashion rote learning and regurgitation that they had no ability to think for themselves, as they would be required to do in the academic world abroad. He would set them projects, and even working together they would have no clue as to how to go about organising themselves and finding out information. So it seemed his tutoring ended up having a methodological basis rather than an emphasis on the subjects.

After sharing stories of our backgrounds and how we came to be there, and having a mutual whinge about the horrors of our teaching experiences so far, we decided that we enjoyed each other's company enough to start meeting regularly, mainly to go to the cinema. This was a new experience for me. There were 2 main cinema complexes in Naplos, one among the shopping streets, and the other down on the sea-front. In both we saw some good films, though it was a bit startling when the film suddenly stopped half way through to allow the audience to nip out for a 'fag break'. I can just imagine the directors being horrified at the atmosphere and artistic progress of their work being treated with such scant regard, in the service of one of Greece's favourite national sports.

CHAPTER 22 - STREET LIFE

It was later October, and I was waiting for signs of Autumn, being rather a fan of this season in the UK. While the light would take on a pleasing golden quality, in town there was nothing of the russet leaves and frosty glinting I was seeking. Clearly I would need to go further afield into more rural climes.

Getting bolder on the bike, I would take off along the coast road round the bay, to the East, the West being the initially industrial end and not so appealing. Lina and I had had a wonderful meal at an *ouzeri* right round on the other side of the bay to the West, from where, by the waterside, we could see the whole of Naplos laid out, with the mountain villages behind forming a fabulous diamond-sprinkled black backdrop. But we had gone in the car, and it was a bit far on the bike.

I certainly found some interesting villages along the way, one with a very good art shop where I purchased crayons and modelling clay. There were numerous eating establishments where I began to try out the delights of grilled octopus. It was a bit alarming the first time I saw someone beating one of these poor creatures on the rocks. Was this to kill them? How brutal! But of course I found out that it is to tenderise them. The modern method is much easier though. Apparently, while freezing has a disastrous effect on something like a cucumber, on an octopus it has the highly beneficial effect of breaking down the tissues and automatically tenderising. I had fallen in love with the octopus stew produced by Nektario's sister on Kalkos, but now the barbecued flavour and crunchier texture of the grilled beast was calling to me. Unfortunately, one day, the retsina had called to me a little too strongly, and I found I had to lie down on the verge above the beach just across the road from the taverna in order to sleep off the effects before cycling home.

For real Autumn colour though, I had to go up to the mountain. This was no journey for the bike, for the road got very steep at the outskirts of town. I presented myself for the bus, and duly arrived in Makrinitsa about midday. Here was architecture, and a feel, quite different from anywhere I had been in Greece. It looked Alpine, composed of tall houses, cream painted, with dark woodwork and overhanging slate roofs. As I had suspected, the village was a bit of a tourist trap. And Christmas was coming, so I went shopping for a few presents, notably a dolphin mobile and a set of miniature doll's furniture. I did not eat out, but bought some pastries and then found a suitable spot from which to paint a scene. I was deep into this when a thought struck me about the bus back. Was I sure about the time? What had that horn been? Could I have made a mistake? I finished and packed up my paints. Then I was horrified to discover that I had indeed blundered over the bus time. That horn had been to call the passengers

to the last bus down the mountain. In vain I fulminated at the stop against the confusing nature of the timetable.

Tired, hungry, I was stuck in the dark with little money after the shopping, less Greek and a feeling of doom. I paced to and fro, raking my hair with worry. Then, suddenly, a car stopped and an English speaker enquired what I was doing. I explained my mistake, and to my great joy the occupants agreed to give me a lift back to Naplos. For this I had to pay by struggling to speak Greek to them. I shudder to think what my efforts must have been like in those days, but they were most encouraging, pleased that I was trying. And of course they were able to indulge their eternal nosiness by finding out all they could about me in the short journey. They gave me some good information too, for there was about to be a major national holiday, 'Oxi Day', 28th October, the commemoration of the bold refusal of President Metaxa to allow the WWII Italian army passage through Greece.

It seemed there would be a big parade along the seafront by all the Naplos schoolchildren. Well, this I had to see, so armed with the camera, I duly turned up in the glorious sunshine, to watch the various schools assembling behind their flag-bearers on the huge landing stage at the Western end of the harbour. The whole of the kilometre long esplanade was lined about 3 deep by Greek parents and grandparents. Then to the strains of marching music, the youth of Naplos came marching along, in white shirts and black trousers and skirts. They looked wonderful and marched well. I was preoccupied with finding some of my *frontistirio* pupils to photograph among the throng, but afterwards what I remembered most was the appearance of these boys and girls as young giants compared to their squat little forebears. Such is the demonstration of the power of better nutrition in recent Greek times.

I surveyed the art work which had nearly cost me a disaster at Makrinitsa. Not brilliant, a bit stiff it was and not quite like Greece. It made me think of France. Oh well, practice makes better even if not perfect. And practice I did, taking my watercolour pencils down to the main promenade area in Naplos, adorned with modern sculptures (sadly themselves adorned with graffiti). These paintings, more drawings really, do capture the feel of the place, the space and the gentle glow in the air. It was a fabulous seafront, well over a kilometre long, very wide, with gardens and these sculptures at the Eastern end, and the rest long and straight (and pedestrianised). Cafes lined one side all along, with apartments above. I was rather saddened to discover that once upon a time all the way I along the front there had been magnificent individual villas in

the neoclassical style. A few survivors could be found in the streets parallel to the front. But the lure of the money to be made from large apartment blocks had led to the villas being sold off for the land to be redeveloped. It sounded like the transformation of Athens from a city of big villas to a concrete jungle, in a desperate bid to house an influx of population from the Turkish territories and rural areas.

While I had no interest in the apartment blocks, I was interested in some of the cafes, notably the Hagen Dasz one, home of my favourite ice cream. But there was something odd about the cafes. They seemed to be almost permanently full young men, well though casually dressed. Were these students? Some of them, maybe, for the University was only along at the end of the sea-front. But there were so many of them. I asked a friend in the Foreign Association, who told me that these were the sons of rich families who did not need to work, being kept by daddy, and who spent their days on meaningless leisure. Well one day, I provided some entertainment for the Hagen Dasz set, for I got myself my favourite pralines and cream (2 balls!). I then proceeded to lounge back in my comfy cane chair and eat this ice cream in as sensual and creatively suggestive a manner as I could manage, with many permutations of the lips and tongue. A strange silence fell over many of the surrounding tables as one by one the young men turned their gaze to my teasing performance. It felt like fun at the time, but later I decided that as a lark it was a bit cheap, and did not cast me in the best light, so it was never repeated. Unlike Maggie, I was never interested in 'toy-boys' anyway, so it was pointless appearing to be 'on the pull'.

Eleni and Theodosia were obsessed with my lack of a man of my own, and Eleni kept saying 'We must find you someone' - but they never did. Richard was my platonic companion, and the only other men I met were the husbands of the women in the Foreign Association. Being single could indeed be a big disadvantage, and I stormed out of more than one taverna after enduring 20 minutes or so of being ignored. But my time was my own, and after years of living without a partner, I wondered if I really wanted a permanent relationship again. My aromatherapist warned me that in her earlier days in Naplos, she had been engaged to a handsome young chap, but thankfully she learned enough Greek before the wedding took place to discover what a life of drudgery she would have had, and broke off the engagement. Happily, her eventual husband's parents seemed a bit more enlightened over how to treat their daughter-in-law.

I certainly did not want a guy as tactless as the husband I encountered at the Foreign Association Bonfire party. This was a splendid occasion with baked potatoes and sausages, a fabulous bonfire, and super fireworks, under a black and starry sky. I had taken Richard along as my companion, 28, quite attractive, but balding and so looking older than his years. Maybe it was unreasonable of me to object to everyone thinking he was my son (could have been I suppose). But I was truly insulted when Andreas enquired how many grandchildren I had. Well really! Although in my late forties I was pretty confident I did not look it, so was highly put out to have Andreas as good as tell me I looked older than that. I gave him a good tongue lashing (how Greek of me!) whereupon he spent the rest of the evening back-pedalling furiously and assuring me that Greek women tend to have their first babies at about 19 and so are often grandmothers by the time they are 40.

It was not only tactless men or insouciant waiters on whom I exercised my wrath. I just could not get the hang of the Greek working hours. Needing to visit an insurance office or such, I would turn up about ten past 2 in the afternoon to find that they had knocked off for the day. The air would be blue outside the door as I hammered on it and stamped and generally cursed the whole nation for irresponsible laziness. How did they ever expect to get any work done? Why preserve this traditional practice in the days of the European Union? Surely the coming of air-conditioning had removed the difficulty of working in the long hot afternoon. I had observed that certain sections of society, like shops, would open again on some evenings, but not so offices.

I was learning more about life in my street. I was invited into my downstairs neighbours' house for lunch of a delicious soup, salad and bread. Needless to say the conversation was limited, but I hope I smiled and nodded appropriately. I discovered they were willing to let me keep my bike in the yard at the side of their house, to which it seemed I had right of access. This was a big improvement on hauling it up the stairs in my place. Although I never invited them back for a meal, I did give them some extra out of one of my recipes - lentil soup I think - when I had made a lot, and they seemed to enjoy this variant on the good old Greek lentil soup/stew *fakes*.

Although I had found a quite acceptable wine at the supermarket on the main road, when I ventured in the other direction down my street I discovered a wholesale wine merchant. I proceeded to turn up regularly to sample their selection, poured on draught into one's own plastic bottles. When it came to the *saxaroplastaio* which sold a bewildering array of cakes of all sizes, I contented myself with window shopping. If I ever succumbed to sweetmeats, it was usually a 'Break' bar with fruit and nuts in a white chocolate variety, rather sickly sweet and reminiscent of solidified condensed milk, the latter a great passion of mine. Mostly, I managed to keep my sweet tooth at bay with low calorie hot chocolate drinks, still bringing them in the suitcase from the UK.

I did try an unfortunate experiment of sampling 'food for free' which was reminiscent of my naïve approach to the raw black olive I had fallen foul of a year before. All along the street were little orange trees, adorned with a tempting number of mandarin-like fruit. Well, it was only a matter of time before curiosity got the better of good sense and I decided to sample one. I really could not believe that a fruit could contain such a huge proportion of seeds in relation to flesh, and such bitter flesh too. I'm not even sure if they would be any good for marmalade as it surely requires some pulp, though the seeds are good for pectin. So I had to accept that they looked very pretty on the trees - ornamental oranges - and went on buying the (delicious) edible ones from the street side traders who set up behind their trucks.

Shopping took a new exciting turn when I set off in a new direction and discovered Lidl. I was familiar with this low priced high quality supermarket in the UK but had not met it in Greece before, there being no branch in Rhodes then. From here, I could get all sorts of cheap alternatives to branded goods, and, best of all, a wonderful liqueur-like 7 star 'Metaxa'-style brandy, for a ridiculously low price. It was a bit risky bringing bags of shopping home on the bike, and especially nerve-wracking when the brandy formed part of it. But trying it on foot was exhausting. It would have been better to make smaller purchases more frequently, but Lidl in the sort of shop where you never know what great offers you are suddenly going to see and need to take advantage of.

At least I had the money to shop now, unlike in Stargos where my credit cards were taking the strain. And it was not just on expeditions that I found attractive goods. Sometimes they would come to me. I was generally driven crazy by the street traders in their vans who patrolled slowly back and forth calling through their microphones about their wares. Frankly the guy who informed me at maximum volume 4 times a minute *'Exo patates! Patates exo!'* (I have potatoes! Potatoes I have!) was in severe danger of being pelted to death with his own merchandise. But there was one trader who caught my eye, and for whom I was lying in wait - the rug man. My flat was decidedly chilly underfoot with its marble composite tiles, and needed a bit of warmth and colour to cheer it up. I could here him coming a few streets away, and watched form the balcony as he approached. I think he was a bit startled as I burst enthusiastically through my front door. It was not long before I was the proud owner of 2 large almost square rugs in terracotta and beige (with spiral border design) for the living room and 3 runners of various lengths in green for bedroom and kitchen. They all came at satisfyingly bargain prices.

A more expensive purchase came my way at Athina's school. One afternoon I was a bit early for my lesson, and discovered Athina being visited by a salesman of leather coats and jackets. I owned a leather jacket, but it was in the UK and anyway it was very '80s in cut, edge to edge with huge shoulders and wide sleeves, so very out of fashion. I took a fancy to a leather parka with fur-trimmed hood and padded lining, suitable for the colder temperatures and waterproof unlike my old black cord duffle coat. Meanwhile Athina, a very large lady, was attempting to find something she liked which would fit her. Now I am even better at spending other people's money for them than I am at spending my own, so, encouraged by my compliments about how it suited her (true), soon Athina was investing in a rather lovely tan suede swing coat which admittedly would not fasten but looked ok. With typical large lady optimism (been there), Athina decided she could not pass it up, and was no doubt going to be able to get into it soon when she lost weight.

My new parka was indeed warm on the bike, but the hood was a bit of a nightmare, for if it was up it tended to fall over my eyes unless I tied the drawstring very tightly round my face, leading to pain and discomfort in no time. So I had to resort to my old jersey balaclava, one of the least flattering garments ever to enter my possession, but a lifesaver to such as me who easily get earache. I liked having the parka's elasticated cuffs into which I could tuck my gloves for extra insulation. Mind you, this made answering the phone while in transit on the bike even more difficult, and my lawyer had the annoying habit of always phoning me on my mobile when I was pedalling home.

Mr D, as I will call him, appeared to keep strange hours, going into the office late in the evening, a practice the prospect of which would give British lawyers a fit of the vapours. He was almost impossible to track down if you wanted to phone him, so I was naturally frantic when the phone rang that I manage to answer it lest I miss the call and the chance to speak to him. It was a nerve-wracking time for us all, for the paperwork preparations were going quite well, but the imponderable was whether or not my father's money would be made available to him in time to pay the balance of the money for the Kalkos house. In retrospect, we had extraordinary faith that it would work, and had taken an enormous risk. So, perched half on and half off the bike in the dark and windy street, I would be reassuring Mr D just to keep doing his bit, all would be fine financially, while privately wondering if we had lost our marbles to get into this venture at all.

CHAPTER 23 - FOUR WHEELS ON MY WAGON

I am not quite sure just what made me feel that buying a car was such an important step in my settling into life in Greece. After all, where I was going eventually, on Kalkos, I would have very limited use for a car, and my visits to Rhodes would hardly be frequent. Very important, for my health and my safety, was to achieve greater comfort on my journeys to and from work. Getting kitted out in my 2 piece nylon waterproof suit before setting off through the pouring rain was an absolute pain. Peeling the soggy thing off, I hoped it would dry a bit before my departure. Worse was the debate about whether it was better to leave it off later rather than insert myself into its clammy interior. Then of course there was the state of the roads, and the hazards of the traffic in the conditions, slippery with reduced visibility. So there existed immediate practical reasons.

But psychologically, there was my British sense that having a car was one of the serious necessities of life, and the thought that I had better go for it while the money was around, especially at what appeared to be rather attractive prices. My

British car had been left at my aunt's house, but I had had to sell it at a loss because of an ironic effect of covering it up. I knew that a cheap plastic cover could do damage to paintwork, so I had covered the car with bed-sheets under the plastic. But sadly, my father and my aunt, confronted with the cover having blown off, put it back on without the sheets, so I was horrified, on taking it off, to find that my beautiful dark green metallic paintwork had acquired a strange blotchy quality. The man I sold it to (who would of course make a vast profit after the re-spray) remarked that I would have been better to leave the car uncovered altogether. So a combination of false economy and lack of communication cost me thousands of pounds, for that man knew a desperate woman when he saw one (and a woman who was getting on a plane a couple of hours later).

I had expected to have quite a good time making enquiries around various car sales places, determined to buy new. It had been evil fun in the UK torturing various benighted car salesmen who would take me out for test drives and try to charm me into signing up. But here in Naplos I was not always getting a very helpful response. Was it somehow unusual to buy a new car, or did they simply not believe a woman on her own would be genuine about doing this? Was it odd to expect a test drive, or, at the very least, an example of the model to study in the showroom? The whole process became tiring and frustrating.

But I had discovered a rather lovely little car, the Mazda Demio, a fairly recent model (and most unfairly not beloved of the British Motoring press, it turned out). Though a bit lacking in the elegant looks department, it seemed both nippy and very adaptable, with seats which bent and flattened in all directions. And better, I had discovered a prince among car salesmen, the long-suffering Dimitris who is probably still blaming me for the extra quota of grey hairs he gained that Autumn.

Now would one not imagine that, were one to turn up at a car showroom with a bundle of cash, the car salesmen would practically orgasm on the spot and roll out the red carpet? Not so here. It seemed that the process was much more complicated than that. Poor Dimitris took my order indeed, but it took so long to process the paperwork that the special offer price on the car had expired by the time I got it. I tried to take issue with this, believing that they should have honoured the price it had been when I ordered it, but to no avail.

First of all, I had to have a tax number. Now admittedly, among the Greek nation, tax avoidance is as natural as breathing, so one can see why the Government would at least want to have records of its citizens, temporary or not. But why did one need this to buy a car? Was it some nationalistic racial thing, with certain sections of the population (probably the Albanians) not being allowed tax numbers and therefore not cars (not legally anyway)?

Fortunately, early on, Athina had fixed me up with her accountant Yiorgos, who was in the process of getting the required tax number. It was good to have help, for one thing one discovers in Greece is that one requires numerous documents to do anything. But everyone who issues these always wants to see the other documents, while in vain one tries to explain the 'chicken and egg' problem. Someone has to be first to issue something. And then there is that compulsion they all have to have your original document in their hands, despite protests that your original degree scroll, birth certificate or whatever is at the British Embassy and they can't have it. Surely this time we would not have the problem I found on Stargos, where Sofia and I had struggled to meet all the requirements for my registration as a teacher, only to be told it was all too late anyway. But Yiorgos, a veteran at this sort of thing, took charge of completing the forms, and hauled me off to the tax office to sign things.

A tax number once gained, the next step was to register through the police as a 5-year resident, with permission to work. This would be needed for buying the house anyway. It was there that I had defeated the Catch 22 of the paper trail, and persuaded the lieutenant to pretend he had seen an original document, when he had in fact photocopied the photocopy. Proud of all this progress, I returned to Dimitris at the car showroom. But now began another long process. We traipsed around various mysterious offices, filling in mysterious forms which we then took to other offices for stamping. This reminded me of the health centre in Stargos, but worse.

Finally, early in December, some 7 weeks after my first innocent visit to the showroom, my car arrived. But I had been adamant. I would not drive the car until it was insured for me. So Dimitris had to deliver it to my house, which he did with a weary uncomprehending resignation. I rushed off to an insurance company and made the happy discovery that Greek car insurance is much cheaper than in the UK. (A few young Greeks, over as students, have risked premature heart attacks over this contrast.)

Then came the big moment. I had to have a go. I chose the daylight, in the quiet afternoon before my lessons, and crawled round a few side streets before parking back at home. But my first night going to work in the car was still terrifying, despite the undoubted assistance given by Naplos's one way system, which, luckily, my time on the bicycle had given me plenty of time to learn. I no doubt infuriated everyone by driving along hunched over the wheel at about 20kph, glancing nervously around me all the time, heart pounding. But over the next few days I got used to it all and was soon bowling along merrily. Perhaps too complacently, for this lessening of fear allowed that strange mental switch dreaded by all British drivers abroad. I reverted. In the dark, coming round a bend out of a one way street, I became British, and found myself on the left, facing traffic which was just about to sweep round the corner. Well, it is an unrewarding task trying to persuade a bunch of Greek motorists in a traffic light queue to budge and let one in, but, mercifully, one of them saw the danger in the situation and reversed enough to let me pull over out of the way. Ever since then, I have been aware that it is when in a one way street that one is most at risk, for then the normal parameters of what everyone else is doing, and the sight of oncoming traffic, have gone, and a spatial short-circuit can happen.

Thank goodness the car and I survived that experience, for I was eager to get out and about in the countryside in my time off. Despite my forays on the bike around the attractive bay area, I had the urge to go further afield, unhampered by the vagaries of the bus services. I set off the next weekend past the end of the bay onto the Pilion peninsula, the great fertile region particularly renowned for its fruit-growing - the orchard of Greece. Its other claim to fame is a bit of a culture shock, for it is a valued centre for skiing. This was strange, to contemplate Greece as a country prone to deep snow, for the general image is of hot sunny beaches. Yet it makes sense, with all those mountains in the North. And of course I had been caught in the snow-melt water at the great beach on Stargos back in February.

I was enjoying my coastal potter, when suddenly I caught sight of something new and worrying. A group of hunters with large rifles was setting off up the slopes from the road. So there were men with guns about. One had to hope that their pursuit of the hapless wildlife (partridges usually I believe) would not lead to stray shots in the wrong direction. It was a strange feeling to get round the coastal road far enough to look over to my old home, Stargos, the clear air making it seem almost close enough to touch. Back in the Spring, I had thought the same, looking over in the other direction.

This was my only long outing in the car before the term ended for Christmas. I was faced with another anxiety. What would happen to my precious new car while I was away in Rhodes and the UK? Luckily, one of my bosses, Athina, lived in a quiet square, with lots of parking readily available, and agreed that I could leave the car there, so she and her family could keep an eye on it. Better than that, they would give me a lift to the station, for I was going to try out the train, a new form of transport for me in Greece. I had been very pleasantly surprised at the reasonable fares, so I treated myself to First Class. Evidently we were in the land of subsidies here. My seat was as comfortable as a favourite armchair, in an un-crowded and impressively clean compartment. The only shame was that I could not admire the countryside as it was dark when we set out. But I read and enjoyed snacks from the buffet trolley during the slow but comfortable journey. I was impressed, especially as I had somehow not expected Greece to have trains, what with all the islands and mountains. This of course underlines both what a country of contrasts it is, and how much I needed enlightening.

Arriving in Athens, I headed for Piraeus and the inter-island ferry, taking the opportunity to study the route taken by the taxi driver to get from the South-bound fly-over to the great port. I knew that at some point I would need to drive my car down from Naplos, and I had no wish to get lost. I realised I would need my wits about me, for one came upon the exit quite suddenly, on a downhill stretch after a long curve. The exit road demanded sudden deceleration, for it corkscrewed down quite steeply to end in a wide but anonymous street. I scanned the area for landmarks. Would I remember the turns the driver took? Signs for Piraeus seemed absent. I had tried to explain to him in my minimal pidgin Greek the nature of my agenda. The upshot seemed to be that once I hit that wide road, as long as I turned left not right, I was almost bound to find myself in Piraeus eventually. I consoled myself that it would be daytime when I did the journey. A bit of research was better than nothing.

At least the ferry trip was pleasant and uneventful, on the 12 hour journey, with me unconscious in my cabin most of the time. I was glad to be refreshed, for I was on an important mission. My trip to Rhodes had been set up in order for me to sign the final contract for the Kalkos house. It was the 21st of December, and the deadline was the 31st, the end of the Greek tax year. There had been a lot of moaning from my lawyer over the timing of all this and the fact that people had to turn out at the office (for many witnesses are needed) in this holiday season. He had been stressed by rushing around getting things together. I was unmoved, for I had learned about this sort of thing. Greeks are not great planners, preferring to leave things till the last minute, when they have to be done in semi-emergency mode (usually with a lot of shouting and arm-waving involved).

The vendor was very keen to look after me, and had paid for my hotel room. My part was to make sure I had the very large cheque with me for the balance, and the large amount of cash to pay the notary, the lawyer and the tax bill. The owners got their cheque, and I got a completion on the house, and the urge to celebrate. This took the form of rushing to a nearby shoe shop and splurging on a pair of improbably high ankle strap patent shoes, about as appropriate for Kalkos as a fur coat. Evidently the excitement had turned on my urge for glamour. But my effort was not over. Sure enough, the next day, off I had to go with the notary to make the rounds of various desks in the tax office, culminating in the handing over of 3.8 million drachmas in purchase tax on the house. Of course we had cheated on the price quoted on the contract, in order to reduce this bill somewhat. It is amazing how one gets pulled into wrongdoing because that is just 'the way things are done'.

Hugely relieved that everything had worked out, and leaving the lawyers to prepare necessary copies of the documents, I got on the plane to Athens and onwards to the UK and finally Edinburgh. I was going to have Christmas with my father, and see some old pals. Dad had said of Kalkos, 'I want to stay here for the rest of my life' so I was going to test him, by travelling back with him, and sending him to stay on his own on the island, until I could get away from teaching in the late Spring. Of course I had no desire to stay on in teaching until the real end of the year, for this would conflict with my season in Kalkos.

My travel company boss had already indicated back in September that he was pleased with my efforts and wanted me to continue. So there was a working future for me on the island, but I had to find out what the timescale had to be. I was certain there would be a conflict, and so it proved when I called him, for I would be needed from late March on the island, in order to check properties and prepare. My New Year passed in celebration of our success with the property, but with an uneasy prospect hanging over me. Although it would be easier on me in some ways to be dishonest with my Naplos bosses, I decided I would not be able to live with myself.

As I waved my father off at the little port, on his way to Kalkos, and got back in the taxi to begin my journey back North, my mood was gloomy. My heart was struggling to maintain the image of a bright hopeful future beyond the daunting obstacle of how I would manage to 'do the right thing'. I had to find the strength to get through the next difficult weeks and months. I looked for support to Susan Jeffers' wonderful book 'Feel the Fear and Do It Anyway' which teaches that the basic aim is to be able to say 'I'll handle it'.

CHAPTER 24 - OUT OF THE BLACK

Back in Naplos, I was facing really cold weather at last, which made me very glad I had bought the car. I also had greater difficulty than ever getting my washing dry. With no washing machine, and no yard to hang things out in, I had no alternative but to wash everything in the shower-room then hang my hand-wrung but still soaking garments out on the balcony. This could make me a bit unpopular with the neighbours, for the water would collect and run off through the balcony drain and drip onto people passing on the street below. Ah, you cry, why did you not go to the launderette? It seems that such a project was beyond me in my new country.

On still nights there would be those black skies sparkling with stars which spoke of black ice on the roads. I had experienced one of these on the bike, with the gorgeous crystal Christmas light necklaces of Naplos echoing the heavenly display, but I too distracted by my frozen nose and ears to appreciate the beauty. I had already experienced how heavy the rain could be in Greece, bringing memories of school Geography lessons, with the Mediterranean climate of hot dry summers and mild wet winters dinned into us. But

I was not quite ready for the accompanying violence of the thunderstorms which hit us in January. Is it the clarity of air, the shape of the landscape or the sheer size of the storm system which makes the lightning so very bright strong and long-lasting, and the thunder so terrifyingly loud? One night, I was truly shaken when the thunderclap produced a shock wave so strong that my big French windows were blown open.

I certainly needed my big petrol heater in the kitchen, which I had now become reasonably adept at operating, dismissing from my mind the number of points at which some disaster might overtake me. I trudged of regularly to the petrol station for supplies, filled it, twiddled with its various settings, and learned the tricks. I had not really thought much of the fact that it had a bit of a crack in the glass at the front, where one opened the door to reach in and light the fumes. But it was another vital piece of information, about air supply, which my landlord had failed to make clear to me and which was nearly to prove the death of me.

On a particularly miserable mid-January afternoon, I was filling in the time before turning up at Athina's school by reading my book. Uncharacteristically, because it was so very cold, I was absolutely hugging the stove, sitting with my legs about 2 feet from the glass front door. Above my head, the big metal pipe chimney led the smoke, and a lot of heat, across the room to vent beside the small side window. If there was any warning, I did not notice it, engrossed as I was in my book. Suddenly, there was a tremendous, 'Whuff!' and simultaneously the front glass of the stove blew out, hitting my leg, and making a round sooty mark on my trousers. I must have leapt back with alacrity, for I somehow escaped the raging flames which started pouring out of the resulting hole. Panic gripped me to a standstill as the cause of the 'Whuff!' became apparent. The great pipe across the ceiling had split its joint, and all over the kitchen, me my books, my rugs, everything, gently descended a black insidious fall of soot. The mess was indescribable, but first I had to deal with the fire danger, and quickly rushed to turn off the valves on the heater. Because of the way these heaters work, it would take some time for it to use up the fuel already fed through, so the flames did not immediately abate.

Though torn about the need to keep an eye on things, I decided it was time to alert the neighbours downstairs. Luckily they were in and I managed to convey the seriousness of the situation and need for immediate action. (My soot-covered appearance no doubt gave them a clue that something bizarre and fire-related was up!) My male neighbour rushed upstairs with me, and we were just in time to see the flames finally flickering to a halt. He checked things over and pronounced that nothing was likely to spontaneously reignite. He went off to consult his wife, and came back with the offer to lend me an oil-filled heater until the *soba* could be repaired or replaced. I accepted with grateful speed, for I knew I would soon freeze with no source of heating.

After he had gone, I looked round despairingly at the patina of soot over everything. This was going to be a long and very difficult task to clean up. And soot! It has to be the very worst substance in the world to deal with: infinitesimally fine in grain, greasy, and uncompromisingly black. I decided I had better warn Athina that I had a problem, but promised still to come to do my lessons. This report would give her time to contact the landlord on my behalf and arrange for him to inspect the situation with a view to a remedy. Needless to say, Athina was most shocked, and set about her communication immediately.

Well, where to start with my black kitchen? First, I had to sweep the floor, for I and my neighbour had already started to tread the greasy blackness to other parts of the flat. Next, I had to rescue the books I was to use that afternoon, which went quite well because of their shiny covers on which the soot could not adhere or leave a stain. I then decided the best thing to do was a preliminary sweep everywhere to pick up all the loose soot which might wander. The serious scrubbing would have to wait, for I was nearly out of time, and I still had my chimney sweep appearance to deal with before venturing out. They say 2 wrongs don't make a right, but somehow the misery of this ghastly task occupied my mind to such an extent that I was never overtaken by the nightmare imaginings I might have had of being ignited and burnt to a crisp.

Athina was a tower of strength, and the normality helped me through what might have been a period of delayed shock. She had fixed an appointment with the landlord for 2 days time, at the weekend when we all had free time, and had agree to be present to translate. So I had a target, to get the place as clean as possible by then. The kitchen surfaces came up surprisingly well though the joints round the handles and the top of the fridge always had a greyish tinge thereafter. My books and papers had only suffered on the top of the piles, so that was quicker than I had feared. The floor seemed to take forever to wash, always producing more black/grey streaks from some unnoticed pocket, but finally I conquered. The worst were the rugs. Of the set of 3 green-patterned ones, I only managed to rescue the smallest one, the others being a sludgy grey mess. My trousers had to be instantly demoted to gardening and decorating kit, but my jumper survived very well.

The weekend came, by which time the other schools knew about my disaster. The landlord was not too happy as he surveyed the mess of broken glass, and the broken pipe joint. The latter could be repaired, luckily, but the heater was a write off. I was getting a huge ticking off for my stupidity in not having a window open to give fresh air feed for the operation of the heater. Well no one had told me this, and I was hardly likely to open a window in the below freezing conditions. The heater had simply run out of oxygen, and, rather like a person yawning when tired to increase the intake of oxygen to the brain, had burst itself apart in an attempt to increase the size of its intake vents. I think I got away without being penalised, and I got a new heater, because the landlord knew that door hatch glass had been broken, and therefore that I could claim that the heater was defective. I was not hugely in love with having another petrol heater after this but I was a bit on the back foot in terms of being able to argue.

After this, I worked like a Trojan, keeping my head down, for I did not want my bosses thinking I was some sort of trouble magnet. And I was being a good girl to somehow defer the worst of the fall-out when I had to make my revelation about leaving the jobs. I had talked to my travel boss and found that I had to be on Kalkos by the end of March at the latest to prepare for the season. That was 2 months before the end of the teaching year, and, woman of honour as I am, I could not go on, saying nothing, then drop a last minute bombshell or suddenly disappear. Theodosia and Eleni may have suspected that I was less than likely to be committed to the job, for they overtly commented, when I told them about the house purchase, 'So you're rich, then?' I chewed over the problem, and my fear of tackling it, till the last week in January, then decided I might as well get it over with, for I was tormenting myself. And the sooner I told them, I reasoned, the sooner my bosses would have the chance to set about finding a replacement.

Oddly enough, I went and had my hair cut on the morning of my confession to Lina. Everyone admired my sharp new image. Maybe there was a 'reverse Samson effect', the lack of long hair giving me courage. Lina was upset and angry, and brushed aside my protests that at least I was giving them fair notice and was not a slave to any job in my life if I wanted to make a change. Well at least I had got the hardest one over with first, only right since she was my main school, and the broker of all the other arrangements. But I did not expect her to speak to the others for me, and she did not.

Eleni and Theodosia were quite nasty about me letting everyone down. They made me feel like an evil person. I was beginning to think that doing the right thing was a bad policy with these people. Tharani, Mina and Athina were all dismayed of course, and Athina admonished me for how upset Lina was. Athina herself obviously appreciated my work, for she had asked me to consider working with her more extensively in the following academic year. I had said I would think about it over Christmas, so it was a double blow to her when I had to reveal that I was leaving. I had told everyone that I had to go in the middle of March. The worst thing was that I had to go back to the schools to work with the kids once everyone knew. I was as low as I could be. In my own interests I had compromised the helpfulness and integrity of my nature. Dad phoned to see how I was.

'Dad, my heart is black!' (Clearly the soot experience had deeply penetrated my psyche.)

'Cheer up, it can't be that bad!' he attempted.

'They are making me feel so awful about letting them down.'

'But you are doing the decent thing with them.'

And so on, with my sister also. My family did their best, but it was another British woman, Eileen, who was married to a Greek and ran her own *frontistirio* who saved me from nervous breakdown over it all. Before I had dropped my bombshell about leaving, I had booked to go to a Burlington Books demonstration lecture mainly targeted at teachers of Michigan classes. It could be interesting, there would be refreshments, and almost certainly some free books to be had. Luckily, I had sat next to Eileen, near the front, though I could feel the baleful stares of Eleni and Theodosia boring into my neck from a few rows back. While we waited for the start of the talk, I told her what I had done, and how I was suffering. Eileen turned to me and said I was not to bother myself any more by being upset. Did I not realise they would have done exactly the same thing to me if it had suited them? Had I not heard that most people in my position tended to flee well before the end of the year, with no honourable word of warning? The black despair in my heart began to lift. She was right. They were a bunch of sharks who had used me while giving me no insurance support and no contract.

'Why are you deserting us?' asked the Michigan class at Eleni and Theodosia's, a question which sent a cold knife through my already tortured conscience. But I need not have worried about continuing to work under these circumstances of moral blackmail. It happened that, far from having any problems finding a teacher to replace me, their major complaint, Lina and Theodosia and Eleni replaced me almost immediately at their schools. It was a good job that I had money behind me or this would have been a financial disaster, especially as I still had rent to pay for the remaining contracted months up to May. Naturally, I was now persona non grata with Glenda, who had attacked me verbally at the Foreign Association as a person of no honour for letting down all these little schools. Well, it proved that they all found their own solutions pretty quickly. More hurtful to me was to hear that Sofia on Stargos was shocked at the situation. I was unhappy with myself for having broken her faith in me.

I did have to attend a de-briefing at Lina's just before leaving, to give Lina a report on the children I had been teaching, which she could pass on to the parents. This was naturally a somewhat tense occasion, during which I did give as one of my reasons for leaving the imposition on me of so many schools to deal with. To this Lina countered, with some justification, that I could and should have objected to this at the beginning. There was no point making an effort to win any argument. Best would be just getting out of the situation with as little stress as possible. Ultimately I was not a slave, and entitled to change a situation for myself that was not congenial to me. But lurking at the back of my conscience was the knowledge that I was not being totally honest, having never intended to stay on in Naplos, though I would have finished the year if I could have.

The small schools, run by Tharani, Mina and Athina decided to keep me on. This worked out well, for the days contracted into Wednesday night till Saturday midday, giving me lots of free time on the other days to make various preparations for the next phase of my life. I speculated on the reasons why the small schools had decided to continue with me. Was it because they would have finished with me early anyway, and there was no point in trying to find another teacher for such a short time? Maybe it was the continuity with the kids. And who knows, in Tharani's case, whether it was my post-Christmas gift of a real haggis, smuggled from Edinburgh at her request, which told in my favour? Whatever their reasons, I was grateful to them for at least some income, and loyalty to the efforts I had put in so far.

The relief of at least settling the situation for the remaining time was enormous, and released a lot of energy in me. I began to focus on my move to Kalkos. I approached various removal men, to be met with incredulity at the very idea. What? Move my stuff down to a small island in the Dodecanese? I did not see why this was so extraordinary, even laughable, in their opinion. This avenue appeared to be closed, which threw me back on my own resources and ingenuity. The chief resource was the car, and I began to assess it seriously as a serial removal van. I was glad I had practiced the route to Piraeus with the taxi driver. I got out my map of Greece, and studied the road from Naplos to Athens. Yes, the road to Kalkos was not straightforward (for one thing being interrupted by a lot of sea) but I was laying my plans. Come what may, I was on my way.

CHAPTER 25 - SPRING REMOVALS

It was a sunny Saturday in February when I began to prepare for my first journey to Piraeus and the inter-island ferry. I would spend Saturday afternoon after my class at Tharani's packing the car with as much stuff as I could, stuff I could do without over the few weeks I had left in Naplos. I caused a lot of interest in the street as I traipsed out with my 2 white plastic drawer units on wheels, my lamps, my suitcase of lighter clothes, the disassembled melamine bookcase and the smaller of my 2 cane storage units. I had wrapped most things in large black plastic sacks for protection and to keep the contents securely in place.

I had put down all the seats and removed various headrests and side bits, in order to make the car as van-like as possible. Well I had never driven a van, and quite honestly had not been a great user of my side mirrors up till then. I was going to be tested on new driving skills as well as the ability to navigate to and through Athens to find an appropriate boat. I had chosen Sunday for the journey, not only because it would give me time to pack on Saturday, drive down and then be back in time for my Wednesday evening class at Mina's, but also because the normal weekday traffic, which I reckoned would be terrifying in Athens, would be absent.

The car had a cassette player and I was equipped with a range of good music, Bach, Beethoven, and my latest acquisition, the 5 piano concertos of Saint Saens. I am ashamed to say that, until I inherited this from my Aunt Moira's collection, I had never known that this composer, known to me for 'The Carnival of the Animals' had such a wide ranging and excellent body of work to his credit. Poor Saint Saens; like Tchaikovsky with 'The Nutcracker', he was endlessly pursued by, and identified with, a piece of work he came to hate. So I made sure the cassettes were accessible on the dash board shelf. I filled the windscreen washer bottle and checked the oil and water. I filled the car with petrol and checked the tyres. This little outing gave me a chance to practice with mirrors only, as I could not see out of the back window, so piled up was the car with stuff.

Later that night, I sat in front of the TV, only half concentrating on the film while I studied the map and what road numbers I had gleaned from it to follow. I had about 320 kilometres to drive from Naplos to Athens and Piraeus. How long would this take? Well, being a bit of a speed-hound meant that I would make good time in the early stages, probably doing about 300 kilometres in 3 hours. So, allowing for a break of half an hour minimum, it would take me nearly 4 hours to reach Athens. At that point, anything could happen, from traffic jams to me getting lost on the complicated route to Piraeus. Therefore, for the last stretch, I had better allow at least an hour, even though it was only about 20 kilometres. I knew the boats tended to leave in the late afternoon or early evening.

Of course, in Greece, the difficulty is the frequent lack of an afternoon as we foreigners know it. The period up till about 2 pm is often still called the morning (being part of the short working day), and by the time the siesta is over at about 5 pm one has started saying *'Kali spera!'* meaning 'Good evening!' The words for 'Good afternoon!' exist (*Kalo apoyevma!'*) but are not much used. But, in typical schizoid fashion, when a Greek talks about 'the afternoon' he frequently means a time around 5 or 6pm, rather than any time after 12 noon as UK people would mean. How to cope in such circumstances? A useful motto is that old Girl Guide one 'Be prepared!' Always expect the unexpected and never forget that the whole country is run on GMT 'Greek Maybe Time'.

Adrenaline ensured I did not sleep very well, and was up betimes, having a hasty breakfast before deciding that the earlier I set off the better on this first venture into unknown territory. I had done all the checks on the car, so I was left to make sure that I myself was as prepared as possible. I checked around for any paperwork I had forgotten, especially my passport, always essential in Greece for we British lack identity cards. Did I have the keys to the Kalkos house? I made some final checks: no lights on, cooker off, windows shut, drinks and snacks taken out of the fridge. My phone and phone charger (so many people forget that) were lodged safely in the bag, where I checked for my money and credit cards. I made a last call to Dad from the landline to tell him my movements. All the time the butterflies in my stomach were hatching out and fluttering around with increasing vigour.

It was nearly 10 o clock, which meant an arrival time in Piraeus of about 3pm. Better get on with it. A last nervous visit to the loo, then down, door locked and soon behind the wheel. The weather was sunny and clear. I put on the music at once, calming my racing brain. I drove cautiously, on the mirrors, through the Sunday-quiet streets to the bypass and so onto the motorway, which was more of a dual carriageway really. Soon, buoyed by Saint Saens, I was bowling along, with hardly another car in sight. The road was good, the visibility great. It was even a little overcast so I was not too dazzled by the sun although I was heading South into its glare.

The road went through beautiful country, through some lovely places, and at times skirted the sea. I had been on the route before of course, when coming up in the bus to Agios Constantinos to get the hydrofoil for Stargos, but it was different to be firstly, going the other way, and, secondly, driving oneself. After 2 hours, I was ready for a break, and spotted a sign for a service station. It was not the one the bus had used, being too far North for the bus journey's break time out of Athens, but I had some idea of how it all worked now. I did find it odd that one had to pay for one's stuff before getting it, having had to decide on it before one had had a proper chance to assess what was there. On this occasion, I had brought food with me, leftovers from the fridge, so I ignored the palatable-looking hot dishes and settled for coffee and (I confess) one of my favourite white 'Break' bars to keep up the comfort-eating part of the expedition.

Venturing into the toilets, I soon discovered that I had to pay the attendant on entry, which was necessary to be issued with what I considered to be an inadequate supply of toilet paper. (Thank goodness for my secret handbag stash!) Worse, I found that every one of the (clean) stalls was a stand-up job. Now I am not inexperienced at peeing out of doors, when it is necessary for us girls to hoik up skirts while keeping knickers out of the way, or perform complex manoeuvres to avoid sprinkling one's trousers and shoes, but somehow, in man-made surroundings, it seemed odd to have to do it. I reminded myself of the horrors of the toilets at Athens Bus Station, and felt I was well off to at least be somewhere which was supervised and cleaned regularly.

On the road again, after a while I saw in the distance some concrete implacements. A toll station was looming up. I groped for my purse to get some change. Ready, I began to slow down, but then my eye was caught by a little figure by the roadside near the pay booths. A little old lady dressed in black, the norm for old ladies in Greece, was holding a basket in one hand and a bunch of small dark red flowers in the other. Anemones are one of the treasures of the Greek Spring, and dark red ones are unusual. I am a kind soul, and if it does not cost much to be nice I will do it. Also, although I am not really superstitious, I had a feeling that being kind to the old lady by buying the flowers would bring me luck on my journey and somehow protect me from mishap. So I invested the modest sum of 500 drachmas (about £1) in a bunch, and was rewarded with a toothless grin and a command '*Sto Kalo!*', ('Go to the good!)

I encountered no more toll stations or flower sellers, and little traffic. In fact I almost had the road to myself until I reached the outskirts of Athens. I was swept along the elevated 3-lane concrete highway, keeping over to the right, for I knew from my practice run in the taxi back before Christmas that the turning for Piraeus came suddenly. Sure enough, after a long bend, there it was rushing towards me. Piling on the anchors, I swooped down the slip road, and tried to remember the way the taxi had turned. I luckily have quite a good visual memory, so I could recognise the look of the roads along which I was travelling. I was very pleased with myself when the proper signs for Piraeus started to appear. But now another problem presented itself. I had not thought much about finding my way to the correct boat. I turned towards the right, in the general direction of boats to the Dodecanese, and decided to park up for a while to investigate the options.

I presented myself in an agency, which had a promising looking poster advertising the DANE line as going to Kalkos. This turned out to be outdated of course, and they could give me no particular help. I tried another agency, who knew nothing of boats to Kalkos. This was frustrating. What I needed was a general information point where they knew about all the boats in the harbour. So, with time going on, I had to make a decision. I got back in the car and headed for the Dodecanese section of the docks. Here I found that 'Dimitroula' was scheduled to leave later that night for Rhodes, the journey taking about 15 hours. Well, that would have to do. I should be able to make it to the afternoon boat to Kalkos. I got a ticket for me and the car, and a cabin. Although inter-island ferries are a very cheap way to travel if you go 'deck' only, I could not afford to be exhausted. After all, I was only spending money I would have spent on a removal firm if I could have found one willing.

Driving into the bowels of the ship and right to the front was quite an experience. They had to put me there, for I would be last off, at the end of all the ports of call. It was a huge cavern, dark and grubby, full of oil slicks and redolent of the diesel fumes of countless lorries, most of them in severe need of a good de-coke. I felt like Orpheus coming out of the Underworld as I picked my way, footsteps echoing, out of the gloomy depths to the passenger stair. I deposited my overnight bag in the cabin (which potentially I would share with 3 other women). Then I set off for a walk around the dock area and beyond, to while away the time till departure.

Imagine my annoyance when I discovered that the big boat which called at Kalkos, 'Vintsenzos Kornaros' was in dock and leaving that very evening, calling in at my island, where I could have driven off with my stuff. The difficulty was that she was in another area of the docks altogether, that for boats going to Crete. I should have remembered that though she went through to Rhodes she was basically a boat concerned mainly with the needs of Crete, connecting that largest of Greek islands to Rhodes and Athens. The only thing with her was that she took 24 hours to get from Piraeus to Kalkos, 26 to get all the way through to Rhodes. Well it was too late to do anything, for my car was now trapped behind a number of large lorries. I would know the next time.

A further blow was soon to fall. The weather forecast had taken an ominous turn, and a prohibition had been issued banning any boats from leaving. As darkness fell, the clouds grew numerous and grey, the wind and the rain got up, and my mood became as gloomy as the weather. What was I to do? What if we did not leave the next day? I was running out of time to get to Kalkos then back to work. The only cheering thing was that the boat acted as my hotel, for they just had to accommodate people who had booked cabins for as long as it all took. 'Dimitroula' was hardly an attractive ship, elderly, rusty, with signs of a more entertaining past in the paddling pool up on the forward top deck. Down by the cabins, the general seediness continued, though the battered old communal toilets and showers were at least clean, as far as I could tell in the dim lighting conditions. (Why is it that the Greeks, who are actually rather good at lighting design, have this contradictory affection for the 40 watt bulb?)

Next morning, Monday, the clouds had gone, the sun was shining, but why were we not under way? The prohibition had been lifted, and the ship I should have been on 'Vintsenzos Kornaros' had left. Almost frantic, I appealed to the purser's desk, to be told that we would set off at 12 noon. Hasty maths confirmed that we would therefore arrive in Rhodes about 3 am on Tuesday morning. What was I to do? I could not go over to Kalkos, for I would have no time to get back up North for work. The only thing was to catch 'Kornaros' from Rhodes, leaving about 4.30 am, calling at Kalkos, and somehow drop the stuff off but stay on the boat myself with the car.

I had often observed people rushing onto these big boats when they came in for the all too brief docking time in Kalkos, and emerging hurriedly with bundles of stuff carried or wheeled by hand or in little trucks. We had a specialist driver, a Georgian, who appeared to take lorries on and off. I resolved to phone Jill and Jenny on Kalkos and see if they could help. This would be quite an act of friendship as the ship came in very early, about 6.45 am, and it would be cold. They agree to help and said they would enlist the help of the transport specialist Gregori, a strong pair of arms, with the use of a little 3 wheeled truck suitable for the paths of Kalkos.

Much relieved that things were settled for now, I decided

to go and amuse myself on shore until departure time. The waterfront at Piraeus is no show place, being composed of a huge dual carriageway, skirting the docks at one side and with concrete blocks of flats and offices on the other. But the next street back was, for a major port, quite attractive, with pleasant tree-filled squares off it and a most impressive church dominating the scene. The time passed quickly, and soon we were getting under way. One of the crew who knew English and that I had been exploring mentioned that if I had been a little earlier on the Sunday I would have been able to go to the excellent street market, held in some side streets near the docks. I made a note of this possibility, to be attempted on my next trip.

I found it rather strange to have a shifting population of women in the cabin with me overnight, for two got off at unknown stops along the way, and others appeared to use the remainder of the 2 bunks. At least I could sleep until the destination. I doubted I could have slept if I had needed to get off at a temporary stop. There was the famous Kalkos story to remember, of the chap who got off 'Kornaros' during her brief visit to the harbour, to get cigarettes from the kiosk (the shop lacking his brand). Up went the gang-plank and off she went, with this poor chap running across the jetty waving and shouting to no avail, for they would never return..(In fact I have seen them return once, for a poor old lady who simply could not get down the stairs from the upper deck in time to get off.) The man's car was on board, so he had to charter the water taxi to Rhodes, get a taxi to the airport and fly to Heraklion, then rush to Agios Nikolaos to catch up with the ship, some 7 hours later, with his pockets many drachmas lighter.

Once roused in the early hours of the morning, and having braved the communal toilets and washroom (no locks, no privacy), I trudged off into he bowels of the ship once more, to retrieve my little car. It was dwarfed by its fume-belching neighbours, whose progress I had to skip around. Thankfully I found enough manoeuvring space to turn round rather than reversing out (never a strong point of my driving). It seemed completely mad to immediately make for the interior of another vessel. I stopped and enquired about tickets, and was pleased to find that they were issuing them there, rather than at some difficult-to-find office, and that I could get on immediately. The final hurdle was persuading the puzzled crewmen that I could not immediately put the car upstairs on the car deck (for 'Kornaros' has a kind of mezzanine with a ramp above the space for lorries.) Somehow, I managed to convey that I had to drop off lots of *pragmata* (things/stuff) in Halki which people would need to get at quickly. So they let me leave the car near the luggage depository and go and relax upstairs (as much as I could with the tension of the next phase).

My heart was pounding as we approached Kalkos. Would my helpers be there? Would it all work out? Worries ran through my head as I got the stuff out of the car in readiness for being collected. But I need not have worried. As the ramp went down, with me standing just inside it, there, expectantly, in the brisk February breeze, stood Jill and Jenny and Gregori, beside the little truck. Jill exclaimed 'Wow you look great!' which I took to be a reference to my new sharp haircut. I hurriedly pressed a set of house keys into Jenny's hand, as the 'team' helped me rush on and off with my things, which they would simply shove into the house. Only 3 minutes had passed since the boat tied up. In those circumstances, it is easy to see why, as soon as the ramp has been lowered, the announcement is made that visitors must go ashore as the ship is ready to sail. Sure enough, the 'ramp up' noise 'Wee-wah wee-wah etc' began, so with a quick shout of fulsome thanks I was engulfed once more in the great metal cavern, and dutifully moved the car to the top deck and my allotted space for getting off at Piraeus.

I slept most of the way back, having been lucky this time in treating myself to a double cabin, and finding to my delight that I was given a key, but no other occupant in the whole journey. I needed that rest, to build myself up for the speedy drive North. All passed quite smoothly, and I arrived on time, if slightly bemused, to take my class at Mina's that evening. Well, I had proved it could be done, even with the obstacles in my way. I was confident of a better experience next time.

CHAPTER 26 - NORTHERN VOYAGES

Once I had completed my first long journey in the car, I seemed to be bitten by the travel bug and had the urge to wander further away from Naplos, now I had the time to do so. I reckoned I had about 2 more trips to do with the car to Kalkos to deal with my stuff. And one of these would be my final one. So the other now very long weekends I could spend exploring. Since I had been South, the obvious direction was North.

It was a clear but fairly chilly late February day when I set off for Thessaloniki, the second city in Greece, and quite a centre for the Arts, I'm told. I was excited that I was going to be passing near the fabled Mount Olympus. As I got near, I worried, as the clouds seem to shroud it, but, having gone past in a fit of disappointment, I glanced in the mirror, to see the clouds had parted and there it was, snow-covered, cone-shaped. I stopped and got out the little single use camera I had been forced to purchase at a service station (fancy forgetting the camera!) So I had seen the HQ of the gods, albeit not at very close range.

I was very impressed with the wonderful ruined Byzantine fortress I was able to go round shortly afterwards, during the brief period of sunshine that day. I spent quite a while scrambling about amid the massive walls and grassy slopes, with their few early Spring flowers. I'm ashamed to say I can't remember its name, but I think Jenny from Kalkos knew it too, and had loved it. Shortly further on, I was amazed to see a motorway sign for Bulgaria! Now, in the UK one is used to signs for Birmingham, York etc but a slip road to another country, that's exciting, and rather scary, as if one could be swept against one's will across the border.

I was beginning to realise that it was no joke, driving North in what was still Winter, certainly in this part of Greece. Exploratory openings of the window produced increasingly icy blasts, and I began bracing myself for the necessary exposure of a tour of the city on foot. I entered Thessaloniki and made my way into the centre, but managed to stop on quite a wide street still just in a residential area, before I got to a parking control district. Rather like Naplos, the city was set along the rim of a bay, though here there was not the dramatic mountain backdrop. It may just have been the freezing weather, but the place seemed very austere, the unadorned apartment blocks along the front, the promenade with statuary but little to soften it. (Was I being unfair? Of course the vegetation would be bare. Did I fail to notice trees and bushes?) The wind was so bitter on the seafront that I had to retreat inland, but not before a rather exciting little incident.

I had noticed as I was walking along a rather large, tiered building looming up. As I got closer, I saw a number of large cars lurking around outside, with chaps in sharp suits clutching 'walkie-talkies' lurking near them. Just as I was about to pass the place, a particularly posh limousine drew up and a couple got out, accompanied by yet more men in suits. It was only after they had set off up the stairs past me that I realised who they were and got off a quick shot (blast, no zoom!). Leader of the Opposition Karamanlis and his wife had just turned up for a speech-giving at the Municipal Hall. What struck me in retrospect was that no one paid any attention to me ditzing around, sort of caught in the wrong place and pointing something at them which could well have been much more damaging than a little single use camera.

I wandered around the seafront and the streets, photographing various attractive statues, and imposing buildings, before succumbing to the biting cold and retreating (to my shame) to the nearest warm spot I could find - Macdonald's. Here I filled up on coffee, burger, apple pie, hot comfort food to sustain me, before deciding I had had enough and would go home early before tiredness added to the hazards of driving in dusk and dark. I send my apologies to Thessaloniki for not giving it a proper chance. I must return in warmer climes to spend a few days sampling the cultural life and the 'real' restaurants.

My next trip in early March was the second one to Kalkos, and went much better. The contents of the car this time were my other, larger cane shelf unit, my personal books, my rugs, the fabric I had bought for craft activities, the artificial flowers and vases, and more lamps, to adorn the Kalkos house, the metal chairs and mirror from the Eastern furniture shop, the folding table, and the shower rails and curtains. I had to be mindful that I needed to get the bed and the bicycle into the last load. And I was leaving a little extra squeezing in room, because I remembered about the wonderful street market I had heard about on my previous trip, and deliberately built in extra time by leaving very early, in order to get to 'Vintsenzos Kornaros' and settle in before checking out the market and bearing whatever booty I might find to the ship in time for the late afternoon departure. The market was extensive, and happily it was a lovely day, so I had a wonderful time pottering around the stalls, coming up with all sorts of stuff, much of it useful, and some just desirable.

I found a great collection of sunglasses, at only 1,000 drachmas (£2) a pair, and bought 3 pairs. I got a bit tired of the cheesy flattery of the salesman who told me I was more beautiful in each succeeding pair I tried on, so I just persuaded him to agree that it was just because I was indeed stunningly beautiful that I would look great in any of them. The purple pair make me look very '60s, and pervert the colours so much that I hardly ever wear them. The graduated ones I reserve for hung-over or post-crying session moments, as they are light enough to see what I am doing inside or at night, and conceal the red puffy or bloodshot appearance. My favourite green ones I wore all the time, but sadly was destined to break them.

My other present to myself was a couple of sweaters, one green, one black, the first rimmed with marabou, the second with Mongolian lamb. I have only worn the second one once, but I soon decided I looked stupid and fat in the first and gave it away to charity. In among this self-indulgence, I found a fabric stall and pounced on some lovely gold and dark blue furnishing fabric, of which I bought a speculative 6 metres each. Those have come in endlessly useful in various guises over the years. The animal print bed-linen and matching fabric did some duty for a while, and still appear as my back up collection.

So shopaholic Fran had had her fix, and I trundled off happily to the ship to stow my purchases in the car. Although I would only have one evening, at least I was able to drive off in Kalkos. Once again, I had a cabin, (this time joined by a lady getting on at Milos) and was getting accustomed to shipboard life, and familiar enough with the simple but wholesome meals to be slightly bored with them. 'Kornaros' delights me because, less well-appointed as she is than some, she looks like a real ship, with rather elegant lines, and the ability to walk all the way round her on a certain level. I did make a bad mistake though, and am lucky still to have my hearing intact (mind you that left ear has been a problem since.) I was, characteristically, pushing out the borders of what I could get away with, and had found a way to get right up on the top deck (normally crew only) as we were coming into Agios Nikolaos in Crete. Suddenly, to my horror and severe aural pain, the ship let off 3 huge blasts on her (very impressive) horn, and I , right in the path of the sound waves, could only clutch at my ears in shock, and vow not to be naughty again. It was a moment reminiscent of the scene in the Dorothy L. Sayers book 'The Nine Tailors' when Lord Peter Wimsey is caught at the top of the bell tower in a church as the huge bells are ringing, and emerges, ears bleeding, but somewhat enlightened about the case.

Early that evening, I drove off in Kalkos, to be greeted by a happy chorus, Phil and Sally among them. His company had so many houses that preparation took ages, so he and Sally had to be there early. Jill lived on the island, except for visits to her family in the UK for about 6 weeks around Christmas, and Jenny was back from her boyfriend's family are in mainland Preveza. I did not have long, but I intended to make the most of it. Part of the strategy involved a bottle of the excellent ersatz 'Metaxa' I had bought from Lidl. Phil and Sally and I retreated to their villa (just at the bottom of the path to my house) after dinner and finished the bottle off between us. Phil immediately christened the 7-star nectar not its real name, 'Anessia', but 'Amnesia'. Still laughing, and with his exhortations to bring more pursuing me up the path, I retired for a brief sleep before catching the boat on her pass through at 06.30, back to Piraeus and my second journey back North.

And North it was I set off on my last trips before I left Naplos. Jenny had often told me of the glories of Ionannina, the city in Epirus set by a lake, where she had spent some time in earlier years. I resolved to try a visit, and soon worked out that the road I would take would pass Meteora, one of the wonders of the World, where monasteries were built on pinnacles of rock, created by the bizarrely different erosion rates of neighbouring geological deposits. In former years, these monasteries could only be reached, or supplied, by hauling everything, people included, up in a 'basket'. This I had to see. But my mistake was to set off a bit late, not allowing for how fascinated I would be by the phenomenon, and how difficult the road ahead would prove to be.

It was now mid-March, and even though the light was getting better, the clocks had not yet changed, and the daylight deserted us about 6 in the evening. I took photos, and clambered around, at the amazing site, my eyes gorging on the organic intricacies of the rock formations, the cunning placement of the buildings, the astonishing other-worldly perspectives created. I took a photo of a Spanish couple atop an outcrop, and they returned the favour. It is one of the few photos of me from this period, and I wince at my unwise choice of the comfy but unflattering green leggings, which don't look as good without the pink socks and boots to balance them. The light was almost gone when I dragged myself back to the car, and set off North.

I hoped to be in Ionannina in a couple of hours, by about 8 pm, but had reckoned without the challenging qualities of the Katara Pass. Although I had studied the map, I had somehow failed to notice, or realise the significance of, the squiggly lines close together with a certain colouration around them. As I got higher in the mountains, I began to see traces of white on the ground, and soon I was worried, for notices warning that vehicles must have snow chains fitted started to appear at the roadside. What was I in for? Would I make it through? Soon afterwards, I saw that the white at the side of the road had changed from streaks to serious banks which had been ploughed up off the road. Was worse to come?

The darkness was almost complete when I reached the first of many sharp and difficult hairpin bends. This would have been difficult enough without the glare of the headlights of huge lorries coming the other way, and threatening to swing out into my path as they ground their way up. The next 2 hours seemed far longer as I climbed to and fro across the mountain, then, mercifully, started the descent on the other side of the summit. Surely I must reach Ionannina soon. But my heart sank as I remembered the map, and the distance between those squiggly lines and the city. I was still in for a long drive in the dark. Finally, about 10 pm, I at last reached the outskirts of Ionannina, the city by the lake. Now I had to find somewhere to stay. I drove into the centre and picked a likely side street to park in. A bit of luck. No parking control. I went into the hotel round the corner. More luck, for they could give me a room for 2 nights. I was too tired to eat, and decided to retire early, the better to explore the next day.

It was a lovely day, in which I wandered all over, from the lakeside, through the elegant squares of the centre, with their almost Baroque-looking buildings, to the narrow cobbled streets of the Byzantine old town. I paused for the inevitable shopping, this time finding an emporium selling cheap socks and tights. But I never was aware of what I was to learn later, that the city is renowned for a particular style of silver jewellery, again with a kind of Baroque look, full of curls and curves in the design. Given my shopping enthusiasm, and the money still in the bank, it is just as well I did not find the silver shops. I decided to take the car up to the major Byzantine site, the huge fortress on the outskirts of town. Unfortunately, at this time of year, the interiors were closed to the public, but I marvelled at the solid buildings, so well-preserved and restored, in the typical strong and squat style. I wandered along the perimeter wall, peering over at the drop and into various ongoing excavations.

Energised and emboldened by this, I decided to explore a bit further out of town and around the lake, getting limpid and misty in the late afternoon. By the time I realised I had to get back, it was getting dark. I came into town by an unusual direction, and suddenly found myself with a problem. I had strayed into the old Byzantine part, where the streets were very narrow, and I had a suspicion I was not supposed to be driving at all. Well it helps to be a foreigner, so I had my 'dumb British blonde' defence at the ready for any enquiring traffic official. Luck was with me though, and I squeaked my way through, to emerge, thankfully, at a location I recognised, and soon had the car parked.

By now, I was ravenous, having just had a bakery snack to top up my hotel breakfast, but I did not feel like straying very far, so I picked the restaurant practically attached to the hotel, where I plumped for a tasty meatball stew, with winter greens. I took a chance on the house red, which was acceptable but not memorable. Altogether, I was very pleased with my visit, not least because of my accidental mini-adventure and my survival of it.

Knowing what I was facing on the drive, I decided to set off reasonably early, so as to be able to allow lots of time, as well as to be able to sightsee in what must be wonderful scenery, totally missed on my outward journey in the dark. Well, the first stage was lovely, leaving the lakeside and the city and climbing steadily to the head of a long valley. I paused on the bare roadside at the top to look back, the far-off lake glinting silver in the strengthening sun. I turned my eyes and the car onwards and upwards, and entered the snow-banked steepness of the pass road.

Let us just say that I am almost glad that I was unable to see anything but the road itself when I was driving over the pass on my arrival. The sheer drops at the side of the road were terrifying. I have a good head for heights, but I was sorely tested. I also worked out that because of the road design, the people going North found their lane to be the one most at risk from the precipices. So it would have been even more daunting in the light than going South. I did not have a chance to admire the stunning views, for my hands gripped the wheel, tension gripped my neck, and luckily my plucky little car gripped the road. And once one had started, there was no respite, for this road had no space for hard shoulders, resting bays or the like. Heaven help anyone who broke down!

At last, much relieved, I was through, and driving on a high plateau which came just to the South of the pass. Here at last I could admire the sparkling snow, the azure sky, but to my even greater delight, here was a sign for a service station. Nerves had made me sweat, but had also excited my bladder, and though I have no compunctions about relieving myself 'en plein air' if needs must, how much better to do so in warmth and comfort. It must have been quite a challenge to run the place away up there, but of course it was a major artery road, however difficult. And the service station was popular. As I pulled into the car park, I found myself among a lot of vehicles, including a coach. Everywhere on posts and trees and pergolas a gorgeous creamy frosting of snow was slowly melting and dripping in the sun. It was a little outpost of civilisation amid the raw landscape. I ventured in, and almost laughed, for the reason for the coach immediately became apparent - a party of Japanese tourists. They say those people get everywhere, but this was stretching a point.

Thankfully, there was no queue at the self-service counter, so I was soon supplied with a rich beef stew with boiled potatoes, and since I could not have alcohol, a treat of rice pudding with cinnamon. The surroundings were warm, rustic, but amusingly international in appearance. Slowly, the Japanese finished their rest stop and began to drift outside whereupon they proceeded to photograph the snow-melt, and each other, against its backdrop, for a few minutes, before piling into the coach and being swept off to their next port of call, which I was guessing was Ionannina. Well at least they did not have to drive through the Katara Pass themselves, but I felt for the coach driver. Needs attended to, I got back in the car and set off, smiling to myself about stereotypes: the Japanese, going all over, with their cameras: the Scots being dour and mean (these people have never met my Dad), and so on. There has to be a reason why people say these things, and I had just seen a demonstration that sometimes stereotypes bear out. The worst of the journey behind me, I made shift back to Naplos and a bit of a rest before my next teaching session the following day.

CHAPTER 27 - COUNTDOWN TO KALKOS

Spring was advancing, the light and the flowers growing, as was my anticipation of my new life on Kalkos. But I might as well enjoy the time left to me in Naplos. Even though I had the car, I made myself go for expeditions on the bike, for fitness reasons, and because it was easier to see more. One of the slightly scarier expeditions was to the hinterland behind the city. I had at last worked out that if I started at the Western end I could get up into the back regions without tackling quite such steep slopes. It was interesting to observe the domestic architecture, having been used to apartment blocks in Stargos and most of Naplos, small farmhouses on the outskirts, and stone houses in Kalkos Here I encountered the bungalow regions of Naplos suburbia.

But close by began another area, far from salubrious, composed of odd little shacks and vans. The gypsy area extended all along the back road, at the very edge of the town. Although a car would have been better than a bike for feeling protected, I was very glad I was not traversing the district on foot, for there were some mean-looking swarthy characters about (and that's just the women!) and a good many doubtfully trustworthy dogs. So I avoided eye contact with anyone and kept up a brisk pace till I had reached the real streets again.

There was a main northerly artery which bisected the great seafront at the bottom, and the parallel streets of the town. Here could be found the main Post Office, the OTE office, and many interesting shops, either on the main road, or on the little streets immediately off it. Here I patronised the haberdashery, acquiring all sort of trimmings and threads for future craft projects, and the art shop where I got some fine acrylics and glass painting materials. It was here also that I managed to beg a visit to the toilet. This was one of the worst things about the city, at least as I knew it. The only public toilets seemed to be down on the promenade, so shoppers higher up either had to sneak into a café, or, more openly, buy a coffee, merely storing up a problem for later. My days on the bike were often spent in some degree of desperation. Once, thankfully at night, I retreated behind the canvas wrappings round a building site and hoped the accusing stream emerging downhill would not lead to discovery. If I was in the car, never easy in the shopping streets, I could at least make use of my emergency potty, a very old bashed stew-pot which I carried for this purpose. I could be observed sitting in the back seat in an unnaturally high up position, my head jammed against the roof, but with an expression of relieved bliss on my face.

The man in the mobile phone shop was sick of seeing me, for I seemed to have a lot of problems with settings and language and so on. And on one occasion I was especially frustrated because the new phone card I bought (a 10,000 drachma one - about £20) had a fault. When I tore off the protective strip on the back to reveal the number I must enter for pay as you go top-up, the numbers peeled off as well. We spent a considerable time trying to decipher what they were from the negative imprint on the strip. In the end, he phoned the company, and gave the long code number of the card. They accepted that it had not been credited already, and put the money on my account. At this point my bad luck seemed to end, and, no doubt to the helpful man's relief, I never had to visit him again.

It was on emerging from his shop one time that I observed an interesting phenomenon. A car was parked, half on the kerb, on this main thoroughfare. It was causing obstruction problems, sitting there with its hazard lights winking. Apparently in Greece there is this theory that if you put your hazards on this makes you invisible to traffic policemen. Quite how one avoids having other motorists running into one's vehicle, given this invisibility, is not explained. Well in this case, the traffic police were indeed gifted with the sight, for one chap was hovering round the car, but he was not (as in Edinburgh) poised to slap a ticket on it. He spent the few minutes when I was in the fish shop pacing up and down by the car, frantically blowing his whistle, presumably to alert the driver to imminent punitive measures. No show. More pacing and whistling went on while I was in the bakery next door. As I unlocked the bike from the lamppost and set off, he was still at it. Presumably there is a time limit on whistling before they tow the car away, but I worked out that probably the guy just did not want to do the paperwork of giving a ticket, or get into the ensuing argument which would only have delayed the removal of the obstruction.

Two wheels can be a blessing in the traffic situation,

and in being able to take short cuts. I had a lovely one along and across the river, from my flat to the Western end of town, where the bus station and railway station were and the docks began. I also used to cheat a bit in the pedestrian precinct and ride along if it was quiet with few shoppers about. I made some strange purchases, I recall. What made me think that huge fake fur coat in grey with black shadow stripes was flattering? I looked like a furry baby elephant in it; another charity shop job. The waterproof duffle which reversed to tiger skin was a natural for me as I'm always a sucker for animal print, but it had to be admitted it was too small for me; I gave it away to a friend. I still have the cool real snakeskin boots I could not resist, even at 40,000 drachmas (£80!). The trouble is, I feel guilty wearing them in these animal protectionist times. The snakeskin effect jeans in matte brown hang in the wardrobe, but the satin finish black and white and grey jaguar patterned ones were just too weird; guess where they went. I would have been better to get another jacket like my wonderful blue brocade tuxedo type, in which I have to say I look the business. It is made of some mysterious substance which never shows dirt and can be jumped up and down on, crushed into a ball etc without showing any creases. It reminds me of that film with Alec Guiness, 'The Man in the White Suit' where he invents this fabric which never gets dirty and never wears out, and is pilloried and attacked (understandably) by all his fellow cloth manufacturers.

My two wheels served me well, but I could not say the same for the motorbikes of Naplos. Eleni and Theodosia's school was on the corner of 2 streets, and my classroom was at the top, just above the uphill corner. We had to have the windows open for ventilation, and the constant noise of bikes revving to get up the hill, pausing, then revving again to set off, was infuriating. The toll taken on my audibility was as nothing to the toll on my nerves, never the most robust part of me. Of course, in the UK this sort of thing would be bad enough, but in Greece there is an extra twist. Since it is very compelling to the young Greek male to make his presence felt acoustically as well as physically, the ability to produce as much growling, attention-getting noise from one's vehicle as possible is very important. A hole in the silencer would be greeted not with dismay but delight, or even deliberately induced as if customising the bike.

Exam time was coming up, and I had to put in an appearance at the exam centre on the day of the orals, for the sake of the Michigan students at Tharani's. I was a bit fearful of encountering Lina or Theodosia and Eleni, but as it happened it was only the latter 2, who contented themselves with a short withering glance and a spell of ignoring. I was delighted, though, when my star pupil came bouncing out to tell me that she had been able to talk about her favourite subject, Ancient Egypt, and had paralysed the examiner with her articulacy. The class had been dominated by this girl who was streets ahead of some of the others. It was hard to draw them out at question time for they would sit back and let the brighter ones do all the work; ever a teacher's problem. I remember a particular discussion, about pollution, which was quite revealing in that it showed that a narrow view was being taken that pollution was chemical. I kept plugging away to get at the ideas that sound and vision came into it too. I must admit that wind turbines are a particular sore point with me, fascinating though they are individually and close to. Greeks, with their noisy lifestyle, are unlikely to be much concerned with aural pollution, while their 'not in my backyard but anywhere else is ok' attitude to rubbish does nothing to improve the unsightly refuse problem.

I was at the end stage now with my teaching, giving reports to my bosses on all the pupils I had taught. The atmosphere was pleasant at all of the schools, and I was left feeling that I had indeed done some good. I had about another week before leaving, and tried hard to come to a suitable breaking off point in the lessons, in all my classes. And I had someone else to say goodbye to also. My only private pupil was Christos, a charming army officer who came to me twice a week for conversation lessons. I felt a bit guilty about him too, for we had not found each other till after Christmas. I had never really considered how to handle such lessons, though I did find a suitable book for us to base ideas on. But often we ended up talking about something else, as Christos would somewhat anxiously remark. My riposte was always that we had been talking, he had been practicing, so what did it matter what the subject was as long as the conversation flowed?

Christos invited me to his home for Sunday lunch one week, picking me up in the car. I insisted we stop at a *saxaroplastaio* because I was well aware of the rules of hospitality which demanded that the guest appear with a present for the household. In the UK I would take alcohol, but in Greece sweets are more the thing, especially as the children, who would certainly be present on this occasion, could participate. It was a slightly awkward occasion, as the wife and children spoke no English and my Greek was very limited. We watched the TV together after lunch, till I felt a decent time had elapsed and made a move to be taken home.

I always had to run the gamut of various sweetmeats when I visited Athina. If it was not doughnuts it was fruit preserved in syrup - so called 'spoon sweets'. Clearly this was a major reason for her large size, and I decided it would not be tactful to protest too much about the fattening offerings for fear of offending her. On my last visit, I talked to her a bit more about my regrets over not being able to settle to the teaching life. I felt I owed her that, for she had been the most helpful to me. I also discussed arrangements to have her sofa bed picked up, the only furniture I had on loan.

Richard and I had had a few more film outings and meals together, notably an occasion when I got invited to join the party by his landlady. I felt I should reciprocate, but in the event only Richard himself came, probably just as well because the seating arrangements were getting difficult since I had removed the iron chairs by now. We were a bit tense with each other, as if he felt likely to get pounced on by me since he had actually ventured alone into my lair. I was faintly irritated at the others for standing me up, and at him for suspecting me of other than simple friendship. Notwithstanding, we decided to plan a final outing together, just before I left. I had been waxing lyrical about the glories of Meteora, so we decided to go on the bus. I had been to the bus station to check the timetable, and all seemed suitably timed for a long day but at least one without the stress of driving.

I should have known, after the Makrinitsa debacle, that I am doomed to be unlucky with Greek buses. But in fact the buses were incidental to this piece of bad luck. Richard and I were equally to blame for totally forgetting that on that Saturday night the clocks changed. Spring had moved forward but we had not. So we both turned up at the bus station to find the only viable bus had departed 45 minutes before. Hastily, we consulted the timetable and found an alternative, though the connection time at Kalambaka, the village just below Meteora, was tight. We had an enjoyable journey, in the March sunshine, passing through the large and rather boring looking city of the plain, Larissa, a major rail junction and crossroads for routes from all directions. We pulled into Kalambaka square, with 2 minutes to go till the departure of the other bus, to Meteora. I could see it across the square.

'Come on, Richard!' I cried, dashing across the square, and approaching the bus, which was now pulling out, from the front. Even though he nearly ran me down, the driver ignored me completely and swept off, the bus nearly empty. I was dumbfounded. How mean was that? And how illogical to abandon potential passengers! Well we had come this far, so we were not to be beaten now. I appealed for help from some locals and was pointed to a taxi. The fare was not too expensive between 2 of us, so we went for it, and soon were peering out as the great rock outcrops we could see from the village got closer and closer.

We started at the top of the winding route, though (wisely) deciding that we did not have time to visit the interior of any of the monasteries. Chatting, marvelling, lingering for photographs, forgetting to allow enough time to do the journey on foot, we left it a bit late to get down for the bus. Despite putting on a lot of speed on the outskirts of the village, it looked like we were going to be stranded. Oh no not again, I thought, at which point we spotted a taxi and piled in. Back on the bus, for the long journey of 3 hours, in the dark, our conversational powers were tested but actually found to be just fine. I of course had had the benefit of bringing up 2 teenage sons so was not too out of touch with modern music, football and the like. And I never tired of hearing Richard's acid descriptions of his students' inadequacies, and his boss's eccentricities. I wish I had kept in touch with him, but some things get lost along the way in life.

My last Northern journey had been made, and now I had to set my sights Southwards once more. I looked round the flat. Hmm. I knew my car was a capacious little treasure, but I was beginning to wonder if I should have paged Dr Who to borrow the Tardis. Well, I am nothing if not determined. I began with the bed (how did I get that mattress in?) then the bike, with its front wheel removed. I worked on steadily, till every chink was filled with clothes and books and cooking pots and sheets, and the televideo and so on. Once again, I was just able to see the vital door mirrors above the piles. It all took a bit longer this time, for I had to clean the flat as well. The landlord had been a bit difficult about how much rent was owed but I was adamant that I had paid enough deposit to consider myself all paid up if I put in one last payment for April, which he got a few days early. Giorgos my accountant had been working away winding up my business, a vital task, for otherwise one can be asked for tax in years to come against a business which no longer exists. (You've got to admire the Machiavellian qualities of the Greek tax authorities.)

It was gone lunchtime before I was satisfied with the state of the place, and handed my keys to the people downstairs, who shared the same landlord. With a last glance up and down the street, I drove off, anxiously calculating as I studied the dashboard clock. Now I had done this journey twice before, with no hitches, but one never knows, and I was setting off later than normal. This time, there was no relaxed break at the service station, just a quick toilet visit and back on the road with the foot to the boards. And just as well, for the traffic in Athens was much heavier than I had met before, being late afternoon when all the trippers and visitors to relatives would be returning home. It took me about 45 minutes instead of 10 to reach the turning for Piraeus. My throat tightened. Surely, I could not fall at the last fence? At last, in the golden light of the sun going down, with half an hour till the 7.30 pm sailing time, I pulled into the dock in front of Kornaros, and rushed to the ticket office. Much relieved, I presented myself to the chap taking the tickets.

'Oh, it's you again! You're late today,' he observed, matily, slapping a sign for Kalkos under the windscreen wiper.

'Well, you know what to do, just get yourself on there!'

I felt part of a big family as I drove up the ramp and let myself be directed into the bays for journey's end. In a few minutes, I was the happy occupant of a nice cabin. I went on deck in the sunset glow to see the last of the loading, and the casting off. Soon, I proceeded to heed the call to the self-service restaurant, which was opening just as the ship pulled out. Made it! One phase of my life was over, and I was on my way back to my island. It is hard to say that I chose the island, for fate took such a hand, and in some ways the island chose me. The story of how I made my life in Greece is one of seizing and following every interesting opportunity which presented itself. When I wrote my description of myself for the Internet recently, I said

'Freedom, and Fun and Beauty. That's Greece, and me!' And you don't get better Greek expectations than that.

Made in the USA